Soviet Media in Transition

Soviet Media in Transition

STRUCTURAL AND ECONOMIC ALTERNATIVES

Elena Androunas

Westport, Connecticut
London

Library of Congress Cataloging-in-Publication Data

Androunas, Elena.
    Soviet media in transition : structural and economic alternatives
    / Elena Androunas.
      p.   cm.
    Includes bibliographical references (p.) and index.
    ISBN 0–275–94147–7 (alk. paper)
    1. Mass media—Soviet Union. 2. Press—Soviet Union. 3. Mass
media—Russia (Federation) I. Title.
  P92.S65A53 1993
  302.23′0947–dc20   93–2862

British Library Cataloguing in Publication Data is available.

Library of Congress Catalog Card Number: 93–2862
ISBN: 0–275–94147–7

First published in 1993

Praeger Publishers, 88 Post Road West, Westport, CT 06881
An imprint of Greenwood Publishing Group, Inc.

Printed in the United States of America

∞™

The paper used in this book complies with the
Permanent Paper Standard issued by the National
Information Standards Organization (Z39.48–1984).

10 9 8 7 6 5 4 3 2 1

CONTENTS

ACKNOWLEDGMENT

I am grateful to the Freedom Forum and the Freedom Forum Media Studies Center, who encouraged me to write this book and made it possible.

INTRODUCTION

The mass media system as an entity has never been a subject of academic research in the Soviet Union. Journalism professors and scholars were allowed to study pieces of the mosaic, but nobody was permitted to analyze the entire picture and discuss it. The prohibition in this sphere—the propaganda machine as such—was among numerous taboos imposed on the country by the Communist system as far back as the 1920s.

Basically, research on journalism here stopped at the level of 1924, when Vladimir Lenin died. Since then not a single new word about the press of this country that would contradict Lenin's theories has been printed. The world has changed, but Lenin, who died long before the contemporary media appeared, is still considered the highest authority in explaining what is going on, as if he were a magician who could really foresee the future. As a result, journalism students in this country have neither a single basic textbook on mass communications nor scholarly books on the Soviet media system as an entity.

Lack of general research was a common problem in all the humanities, of course, though the situation in journalism studies might be the worst because of strict ideological supervision. All research in the society was framed and limited in such a way that it could not deal with the basic principles of the system—it was supposed that the classics of Marxism-Leninism had already stated everything. The major scholarly efforts were directed to prove the veracity of the Marxist dogma. This included media studies. If reality did not correspond to the theory, so much the worse for reality. The whole country lived as if behind a looking glass of Communist dogma.

When perestroika began and an adequate understanding of the state of the society became a vital necessity, even the highest echelons of power did not possess the required data. Everything was unclear: not only where to go but where we are starting, and what kind of a society we are living in. Labeling it "developed socialism" or "the first stage of communism" was the privilege of the highest Party leadership, but those labels had no relation to the realities of the system.

In the mass media, as in the other fields, absence of a system for analyzing the society has created and keeps creating many difficulties, both in selecting ways for developing (or radically reforming) the media and in interpreting the concrete processes that prevail in the media now.

Although different problems of the media are often discussed now, those deliberations are mostly limited to details, such as the price of newsprint, controversial television programs, and starting new publications. The system itself has not yet become a subject of public or political debate, or of scholarly analysis. This approach to the media as a number of entities and problems has proved unproductive. It originated with perestroika, the purpose of which was to improve some characteristics of socialism but not to question the system as a whole. These piecemeal methods were also encouraged by the special stature of the media as an element in the management of the society.

A schema for analyzing the mass media in the Soviet Union is needed to interpret the transformation of the media system from an element of the Party power machine to that of a state machine. It will also help us to evaluate the possible variants for restructuring of this system. The schema offered here is an analysis of the media system in the context of the political, economic, and ethnic developments under perestroika of the Soviet society.

The mass media of the Soviet Union were instrumental in the radical changes that shook the country. They roused the people and generated wide popular support for the democratic movement that overpowered the ruling mechanism of the Communist system. It was a dialectic process: by liberating themselves, the mass media were bringing about the liberation of the people and the people in turn demanded freedom of the press and supported independent media voices.

The mass media role is vital everywhere, but in Soviet society it has been especially important. The media were an integral element of the totalitarian system, the most powerful weapon of an all-pervasive brainwashing complex.

It is no wonder that Michail Gorbachev started his restructuring of the country by creating a new political and ideological environment for the press: glasnost. His predecessors used the news media to preserve the system; he used them to reform it. Without them nothing would have happened. As a junction of ideological, political, and economic issues, the mass media present a unique reflection of the society in transition.

The news media were instrumental in perestroika and their development within those years is a fascinating story of a search for a new identity and a new role in a changing society. The ideal of freedom of the press that emerged under glasnost was the strongest incentive of that search.

This book has been influenced by four major principles that are crucial for analysis of the mass media evolution under perestroika.

1. The first is a notion of the former Soviet Union as a very stable, conservative, deeply rooted ideological, political, social, and economic system. It will take decades to restructure it completely, although the Communist party has collapsed and the Union itself has disintegrated. The mass media are an element of this society experiencing a dramatic evolution. The society that has been living under the pressure of a totalitarian Communist regime for seventy years is now attempting a painful transformation to democracy in politics and a free market in economics.

But the attempt to liberate itself from the past has been successful only to a certain extent. In fact, we now have a number of replicas of the old Soviet Union. However different they may appear at first glance, all of them reproduce the distinguishing features of the system they originated from. In this sense although the Union itself has disintegrated, an innate "Soviet" characteristic is still a component of the new sovereign states and their mass media.

2. The second basic principle is a consideration of the problems of press freedom, of creation and development of independent mass media in the context of political confrontation not between the left and the right (besides, the Soviet political meaning of those terms is different from that in the West), but primarily between the establishment and the opposition forces.

This approach has been conditioned by the dominant role that the Communist party and the state have normally played in the sphere of the mass media. The government, as a result of perestroika, has inherited from the Communist party authority over the entire mass media system. This means that, in the absence of strong democratic traditions, the level of press freedom and degree of state interference in the mass media are fully determined by the political forces that in this particular period exercise complete power in the country. They don't only regulate the media system; they control the predominant part of it. The politics of the state in the mass media field is the most telling indicator of the real intentions of the powers that be and their attitudes toward pluralism and democracy irrespective of their rhetoric.

3. The third basic principle is rejection of any ideological dogma as a cornerstone of mass media analysis and reliance on the Western understanding of the media as business entities. Notions of an "owner" and "ownership" are at the core of it, and they determine both the system itself and its relationships with the other institutions of the society.

In this country where everything used to be controlled either by the

Communist party (which has collapsed) or by the government (of a country that has disintegrated) the question, Who owns?, is not always easy to answer.

The Soviet mass media legislation avoids the notion of "ownership." This legislative vacuum produces some controversial results, including a tendency for expropriation. Most of the media are state controlled, very few are private, some belong to public organizations. There is still much ambiguity around the term *ownership* in the mass media, and private ownership has not yet been fully legalized in this sphere because of the resistance of the old ideological forms.

But ideology is just one reason. Another is the fact that in reality there are no large owners in this field (or in the other areas of the economy) that could effectively compete with the state. Like any monopolist, the state would prefer that people not realize how powerful it is. For as long as the state is dominant in the media area, this hypocrisy will continue.

4. The fourth point that determines our analysis of mass media development is the dominance of the "lumpen" ideology. It has become quite obvious by now that the increasing difficulties the country has been experiencing within the last several years are not just problems of incompetent government or paralysis of state power. These are also (and probably basically) problems resulting from seventy years of Communist rule, which fostered a widespread "lumpen" ideology, which tried to reduce all society to the lowest common denominator. It also reinforced negative attitudes toward private ownership.

But probably the most striking and devastating legacy of this rule is the reduction of cultural and intellectual expression in the public realm; this is a crucial problem for the media.

Taken together these factors form a highly unfavorable political, economic, social, cultural, and intellectual environment for all kinds of reforms that have been introduced in this country since 1985, including reforms in the mass media. These objective circumstances determined the course of developments and their rapidity as well.

But subjective circumstances were also very important. It was a matter of the goals that the highest leadership of the country actually aimed at before the August 1991 putsch. During all those years the officially stated objective of the policy of perestroika was to improve ("reform") the system, not to replace it. The changes in mass media, however radical they may be, have also been limited by the general course of the reforms.

Soviet Media in Transition

1

NEWS MEDIA AND PERESTROIKA

THE MEDIA AND THE POLICY OF GLASNOST: FROM "SOCIALIST PLURALISM" TO FREEDOM OF THE PRESS

Until recently the mass media in the Soviet Union have never been considered newsworthy in themselves. Coverage of the media on the national level was limited mostly to periodic reviews of the press and television in *Pravda*. *Pravda* issued darts and laurels; evaluations were primarily based on ideological and sometimes (in the case of TV) artistic standards. Journalists and editors facing this kind of review were defenseless because nothing pronounced by the establishment media, the voice of the highest Communist party authorities, might be criticized or disputed—it was a verdict that could never be challenged. Those realities were reflected in a sad joke that used to be popular among journalists in the Soviet Union: Every editor in the country can publish anything he or she likes but only once in a lifetime.

As to the media system itself, it was never even discussed in this style of rule. It had to be taken as a given and stayed basically unchanged and unchallenged for decades. So it is no wonder that it has not been a subject of news coverage, even less of debate.

The struggle for power that was unloosed by perestroika changed the situation absolutely. The media turned out to be at the very center of the turmoil; they were both weapons in this fight and some of its principal objects. It is quite understandable that now they are a subject of news coverage almost every day. Some political forces try to secure them in their domain, including control over the media system, and others contend for their share of influence.

This contradiction is distinctly reflected by the fact that different elements of the media structure are subject to criticism from different sectors of the political spectrum. For instance, television is rarely criticized by the authorities, with the rare exception of a few programs that are considered too liberal. This is understandable: the state TV is a part of the power structure. At the same time the active opposition forces question the TV system itself and apply for their share of the existing channels or for alternative ones.

On the other hand, the press is now rather diversified and official criticism is directed primarily at opposition publications, which sometimes they attract even larger audiences and the widest public endorsement as a result of that condemnation.

Today the mass media of this country are on their way to establishment of freedom of the press. The process is neither quick nor easy. It has been conditioned by a very complex combination of political, economic, social, and ethnic factors. The dynamics of the process can be presented in the most general manner as the following sequence of developments:

1. At the start of perestroika the entire media system was under the tough overwhelming control of the Communist party.

2. Glasnost was allowed as an instrument of Michail Gorbachev's policy of "improving socialism" and a weapon of his struggle against orthodox Communists and the party nomenklatura.

3. Glasnost weakened the Communist party's control over the media. Development of the so-called socialist plurality—plurality within the frame-work of Communist ideology—became the first stage of democratizing the mass media.

4. The declining Communist party was deprived of its constitutional right to rule the country. The functions of supervision over the mass media were taken over from the weakening party by the strong state headed by the Communists. The Law on the Press fixed the new role of the state instead of the party as the principal regulator of the media.

5. Control by the Communist government weakened in its struggle against the democratic opposition. This balance of the political forces when none of them was strong enough to exercise the dominant influence was most favorable to freedom of the press. The balance was broken by the putsch in August 1991.

6. A strong government enjoying wide popular support came to power in Russia under democratic and anti-Communist slogans. It faced no serious opposition. In exercising its authority over the mass media, it demonstrated relapses into the Communist mentality, an effort to control freedom of the press.

7. The government is weakening because of its failure to improve the economic situation. The opposition is starting to grow and organize. The climate for press freedom is improving again.

The USSR and post-USSR movement for freedom of the press was not a conscious choice of the society, or at least it wasn't a choice of a substantial part of it. It was the result of a constantly changing balance of the political forces that are in power and have all the might of the state at their disposal, on the one hand, and opposition groups, on the other.

Such an approach to the evaluation of the forces determining media development is justified by the fact that in this country for about seventy years being in power has meant exercising full control over the mass media and public opinion. Power changes but the tradition remains, though not as strong as it used to be. From this point of view the situation most favorable to freedom of the press is a relative balance of establishment and opposition forces.

The only period that appears to be an exception was the very beginning of perestroika, when Gorbachev, who enjoyed full authority over the country and faced no opposition, used glasnost to promote his ideas. But the seeming absence of opposition at that time is misleading. Gorbachev actually stood alone with just a small group of supporters against numerous and mighty party nomenklatura. Usually it is well disciplined and obedient. But when it feels its interests threatened, it can become dangerous. The lesson of Nikita Khruschev is very instructive in this respect.

In declaring glasnost Michail Gorbachev did not mean freedom of the press as it is understood in Western democracies (let us keep in mind that he resigned from the post of the secretary general of the Communist party only after the August putsch). He intended to use the mass media in his struggle against hardliners in the upper echelons of power and to ensure wide public support for his reforms. Besides, relaxation of Communist party control over the media, however limited at the beginning, had a value of its own as one of the directions of Gorbachev's reforms.

By adding the adjective *socialist* to proclaimed "pluralism," Michail Gorbachev set strict limits on glasnost. It is typical that although he never spoke against more conservative publications during the early years of perestroika, he often criticized those that were the most consistent and devoted adherents of his politics—*Moscow news*, *Argumenti i facti*, and *Ogonyok*.

But the reaction to this criticizm was quite different from what it used to be before perestroika. After Michail Gorbachev criticized *Argumenti i fakti* and its editor at a meeting of the heads of ideological institutions (the mass media are among them), one member of the government attempted to change the paper's management and its affiliation. Leonid Kravchenko, at that time director general of the TASS news agency, made an offer to the Znanie (Knowledge) Society, the publisher of the newspaper, to put it under the auspices of his agency but was refused.

Previously a situation like that would have been no problem at all. The dismissal of an editor who did not satisfy officialdom would be a banality. But thanks to the newspaper readers, the officials failed to achieve their goals. Furthermore, the newspaper gained circulation up to probably the highest level in the world (over 33 million copies in 1990), and five of its journalists were elected members of the Russian Parliament.

Michail Gorbachev evidently meant to use the liberal media as instruments of his reforms, but not to relinquish control of them or allow them to determine their own politics. Nevertheless, the process of liberation had started. It was not always consistent; it often suffered digressions and defeats. But in spite of all the difficulties and resistance by the party and government elite, the boundaries of freedom were constantly expanding.

Glasnost helped to bring together and organize the democratic opposition to the Communist party and the state it controlled that later came to power. Glasnost formed a new climate in the society by allowing people to say what they thought, Glasnost opened new ways for the society by demonstrating the advantages of other political and economic models that were previously concealed, Glasnost by no means was an equivalent of press freedom but paved the road to it.

A point of comparative equality of the forces of the declining Communist power and the rising might of the opposition was reached in the summer of 1991. But in the aftermath of the August putsch, this equilibrium was destroyed. An aborted attempt to restore full Communist control over the country turned out to be fatal for the party itself. Of course, Communism as an ideology could not be fully defeated. But organizational structures that might form the basis for a strong and effective opposition were suspended.

The mass media that supported the putschists, including *Pravda*, were banned, too. By doing this, Russian President Boris Yeltsin exactly duplicated the junta's handling of the democratic media, thus showing a continuity with Communist traditions. Several weeks later the ban was lifted and the newspapers, which formally changed their affiliation, renewed publication. As to the Communist party, its activities were entirely prohibited. Those measures taken by the winners constituted a serious warning that democratic values and methods had not yet been learned by the new authorities.

The destruction of the opposition and imbalance of political powers that resulted from it also were not favorable to the government that established itself by those means. Any power is prone to abuse. Lack of effective control by an opposition creates an illusion of omnipotence that is especially dangerous in this country, with its totalitarian past that has not yet been overcome. The temptation to supervise mass media the same way one's predecessors did is too strong. But it is encouraging, at the present stage of the development of the society, that the mass media cannot be silenced as they used to be.

The new democratic power has inherited from the Communist authorities the system of establishment media with the exception of a few of the most hardline newspapers—*Pravda, Sovetskaya Rossiya, Rabochaya tribuna.* In part it formally inherited state ownership—of national TV and radio and news agencies. But what is really phenomenal and very illustrative of the customary relations of the media and the power in this country, the new government has inherited the loyalty of most of the news media to the powers that be, regardless of their affiliation or whom they supported before, Yeltsin or Gorbachev.

The national TV, which used to be designated Presidential (Gorbachev's) by its management, can now be named in the same way, but referring to Yeltsin. *Izvestiya*, which used to be affiliated with the Soviet legislature, demonstrates the highest degree of loyalty to Yeltsin and his government: It has become popular to support the winner. To some extent this kind of the media conduct was motivated by the media policies of the Russian legislature and government, which displayed intolerance of political dissidents and promoted loyalty and obedience to the state power.

These developments demonstrated that, on one hand, the state institutions in this country, although they can call themselves democratic, are not always friendly to the idea of press freedom. On the other hand, freedom has not yet become a natural state of mind in the news media and the long-prevalent pattern (no other pattern was allowed) of media identification with the powers that be continues.

THE MEDIA AND THE NEW POLITICAL FORCES

In this country the official structure has long been a monolith without permitted deviations or even shades of difference. The notion of a constant open competition of political forces as in a natural state of society had been outlawed by the end of the 1920s. Public political struggle was suppressed by the most effective means—by murdering the political opponents of the ruling party. After that time that tradition of political opposition was forgotten, and by the start of perestroika living generations had hardly any idea of what such opposition entailed. In the late 1980s, a normal political landscape started to form from a zero point.

In the political context of the Soviet Union and its ancestors, the terms *left* and *right* have a meaning somewhat different from that in the United States. There are different reasons for this. One reason is that for a long time our countries have been adversaries confronting each other; the values and notions of one side were reflected by the other as in a mirror where what was left becomes right. In the political spectrum of the United States, Communists are considered far left whereas in the public opinion of this country in time of perestroika, they were definitely right. That is why using these terms *left* and *right* can be misleading.

It seems to be more correct to talk about *conservatives*, meaning pro-Communist forces, and *liberals* or *democrats*, indicating their strongest political opponents, who brought about radical changes in the political system of this country.

But it is important to notice that in the specific circumstances of this country, the democratic movement emerged not as an opposition party to the Communist movement, but from inside it, as an attempt to "improve socialism," to liberalize the system. It was initiated by Michail Gorbachev and a group of his colleagues: Alexandr Yakovlev, Edward Shevardnadze, and some others.

It was a contradictory, paradoxical, and even dramatic situation: the leadership of the ruling party began to create an opposition to itself. Of course it was not a conscious intention. But in a short while, the limits of democratic change that had been created inside the party, became too narrow for the new movement. Because the movement was widening and because the resistance of the party nomenklatura was growing, the potential for democratic change inside the party was exhausted very quickly. Its leaders at all levels of the party structure came to realize that what they faced was not just a new slogan but a real threat to their prosperity and for the very existence of the entire totalitarian power structure that they piloted.

As a result, the party as a whole dissociated itself from the democratic movement and the movement split from it. But the situation was still ambiguous, because Gorbachev, an acknowledged leader of the democratic movement, was at the same time the secretary general of the very party that had actually rejected radical change. In fact, Gorbachev's politics became a constant balancing of those two major political forces. He attempted to make one of them accept more radical changes while trying to slow the pace of creation and fulfillment of the other. He might have hoped that he could bring them together at some point. But he failed. The Communist party proved to be unreformable and unable to accept democratic values. The democrats put forward a new leader.

It was an irony of political fortune that Gorbachev literally created for himself his strongest political rival. Boris Yeltsin, one of the most active supporters of Gorbachev, had only one point of difference with him: he insisted on accelerating the pace of Gorbachev's reforms.

Although glasnost had already been declared, criticism of the highest echelon of power had not yet become permissible or tolerable. At that point, socialism as an ideology and a political force was quite strong. It did not allow even the slightest disagreement, not to mention opposition.

In his career, Gorbachev often had to make choices between the Communist party and the democrats (usually not for the latter). But at the beginning of perestroika the "socialist choice" had not yet been questioned. So, in 1987 Yeltsin was rejected not because of his political views but because he interpreted the new motto "glasnost" too literally and criticized the highest ranking official, violating one of the most deeply rooted taboos of the system.

Yeltsin was dismissed from his positions as the first secretary of the Moscow Party Committee and a candidate member of the Politburo. It was at this stage that public opinion became very favorable to him. His rejection by the Communist party made him a victim of the system. Only then did Yeltsin start to develop into a leader of the democratic movement.

Most of the other prominent democrats of today were members of the Communist party and even occupied high posts in it. There is nothing encouraging about this, of course; it is just the reality of this country. For seventy years, no other political organizations were allowed, and even perestroika was initiated by its leadership.

It is not easy for the Western mentality to understand the role of the Communist party in this country because it was not a political party in the Western sense. Although the party was based on a dogmatic, very narrowly defined ideological foundation, in fact it was not a union of like-minded people but a kind of church. People belonged to it, observed its rituals, and demonstrated loyalty to it because for the most active and ambitious part of the society it was the only way to realize their potential. There can be different points of view on whether it was good or bad, moral or immoral, but as a matter of fact these were generally people of action, many of them leaders by nature. They had become used to doing something constructive and this experience was very important.

This explains why most of the leaders of the new wave in different sectors of the political spectrum are former Communist party members, not dissidents. Dissidents' mission was destruction of the old system. They had neither positive experience nor a positive program. Their organizational weakness and lack of popular support were other disadvantages. The dissident press was unknown beyond a very narrow circle of intellectuals. As a result, dissidents could not and did not play any significant role in recent political developments. An exception, and a very embarrassing one, was Zviad Gamsakhurdia, who was elected president of Georgia. The regime he established was close to dictatorship and it did not last long. Gamsakhurdia was overthrown.

Loosening of ideological control under Gorbachev first brought about the development inside the party of some variant of socialist reformism; later it led to liberal democratic platforms. The logical outcome of this line of liberation from dogma was the ultimate rejection of Communism.

Different people, both rank and file party members and nomenklatura, made their own choices, from orthodox Communism to anti-Communism. A predominant segment of the present democratic nomenklatura is deeply rooted in socialism, in the sense that it was raised by the system and inevitably bears some of its characteristic features. Regardless of good intentions, this inheritance will keep influencing the political thinking and behavior of the new democratic leaders for a long time.

President Yeltsin is probably the best example of a democrat who occasionally experiences relapses to the totalitarian past. Suspension of the Communist newspapers after the aborted coup in August 1991 was one of them; the entire prohibition of the party was another.

His manner of dealing with the mass media also reflects the habits of an apparatchik. After the official visits to Great Britain, the United States, and Canada he had a meeting with representatives of some media "to discuss the results of the visits," as the official account stated. The president didn't invite the journalists who wrote about foreign politics; that would be natural. He spoke to editors-in-chief of a number of newspapers and chairmen of the two state TV and radio companies.

As a result, the event didn't look like a briefing in a democratic country but like the old-style instructional meetings the ideological authorities used to hold with editors. The aim of those meetings was not to distribute information but to give commands on how to interpret events and conduct propaganda campaigns. It was natural that editors and not journalists were in the audiences. These meetings were designed to keep the media within strict ideological limits.

What was in President Yeltsin's mind during his meeting with the editors? And how did the editors feel about it? Do both sides hope that they will be able to continue the old forms between the power and the media and not their content? The problem exists, but it seems that neither side recognizes it, much less tries to solve it.

The fact that the economic difficulties of the mass media were also discussed at the meeting is additional evidence that old habits survive. The editors stand for the free press in their newspapers. But it appears that they do not realize that there are no free lunches, and all the favors they can get from the government will have to be paid back in full—by loyalty, by support. What does all this have to do with democratic understanding of press freedom by a Western editor or a media owner? Economic independence is its cornerstone, and until it becomes a popular idea among the media people in this country, we will never have a genuinely free press.

There was one more peculiar aspect of this particular meeting. Editors of the former newspapers of the Communist party were not invited. This meant that access to information was limited again, as it used to be, and that personal communication with the president was not guaranteed to the press in general but rewarded only to those who deserve it. Later on this nomenklatura style of dealing with the media by Yeltsin's government kept prevailing, although its forms were not always as open as at the beginning of his presidency. But during political clashes, the president did not hesitate to summon his media supporters (of supposedly free and independent media!) to discuss propaganda campaigns for his causes. In April 1993, two weeks before a referendum to indicate whether he still had popular support, the president, as the official information said, met with the leaders of the mass media. But not a single representative of opposition newspapers was invited—only those who unreservedly supported Yeltsin. Among them, ironically, were people with a very wide experience in communist propaganda campaigns, including Michail Poltoranin (head of the Federal information center, a propaganda agency of the government), who used to be a correspondent of *Pravda* and editor in chief of *Moskovskaya pravda*, along with other well known communist ideologists. They discussed how to improve the president's image and to increase his popular rating. The meeting was broadcast by the first national channel on April 9, and the rhetoric of the participants of the discussion was strikingly reminiscent of a routine Communist party meeting. It seemed not to occur to the editors that this openly declared allegiance to the president's cause was a compromise of press freedom.

The coalition of president's supporters is not stable. But for Yeltsin, who is introducing unpopular measures to reform the economy, lack of a dependable and well organized foundation of support may be disastrous.

The democratic movement that brought Yeltsin to power and the Communist party, which has broken up into groups of different shades, are the two most visible forces. But the political spectrum is much wider, of course, from anarchists to Christian democrats, from monarchists to fascists.

According to the press law, the new political parties have the right to publish their own newspapers, and they do. But because of lack of wide reader support and financial resources most are small sheets that do not appear regularly and have very limited circulation. None of them is a commercial success. The publications of the parties are not very numerous either. One reason is that the most of the parties do not have many supporters. Another is that under the communist regime the media focussed largely on politics and ideology. Now that people have a choice, they prefer publications that satisfy their personal interests and needs. One of the first and largest of party newspapers, *Demokraticheskaya Rossiya*. was launched in 1990 by a coalition of parties and movements under the same name and closed early in 1992. Disagreements within the coalition had played a role in the closing, as well as the problems of the newspaper itself.

There are at least two major reasons for poor performance of these party newspapers. One is an evident lack of social basis, which is not surprising when we take into consideration why and how these parties were organized. They appeared not because some social group or stratum needed a party to express its interests but because several people sharing the same ideas came together to declare them. Of course this may be a way of creating a political party, too. But it will be a long time until the organization can find more or less substantial support if it ever does.

There are no precise data on the membership of the new parties but it is usually several hundred to several thousand. The minimum membership required for registration of a party is 5000. In Russia by spring 1991 only four parties met the requirement: Communist, Democratic, Christian-Democratic, and Social-Democratic. Under these conditions it is no wonder that different split-offs of the former 19 million member Communist party, whatever they call themselves now, are still the most numerous and best organized.

It is also highly important that this party had more than enough time and opportunity to hide at least some part of its financial resources in commercial structures. Now those investments can be secretly used to support neo-Communist parties, while their competitors suffer from lack of resources.

The second reason is that the public is fed up with the many years of direct ideology and propaganda imposed on it. In the newly emerged newspaper market, people choose something different, something that may satisfy their personal demands and wishes, which were previously ignored by the official propaganda machine. At the very beginning, people enjoyed Soviet-style muckraking journalism that uncovered the hidden aspects of the history of the system and crimes of its rulers.

The first period of glasnost, when alternatives to the mainstream media were scarce and people felt like reading everything new that was published, is over. Now the reading public has many more choices and is much more selective. From the point of view of journalistic quality, party newspapers are not attractive enough either.

Most of the new parties are not very visible. Their own media are weak and the establishment media, whether Gorbachev's or Yeltsin's, generally ignore them. There are parties, although they are small, that have weighty programs and can be serious opponents in the public debates on today's problems and Russia's political future. But the establishment Russian media keep them silent.

On a regular basis the media report on various gatherings of Communist groups that are trying to restore their party in one form or another. They generate publicity for the very active leader of the Liberal Democratic party Vladimir Zhirinovsky, whose views are close to fascist. At the moment neither the defeated Communists nor the outrageous Zhirinovsky looks like serious opposition and journalists enjoy ridiculing them. Of course this attitude may be not farsighted but that is another problem.

The other parties are ignored. Political culture in this country has not yet developed to the point where the realization that opposition is a natural and necessary element of the political scene is common among the citizens or at least among politicians.

What is actually going on is that the media avoid serious discussions with political forces that can offer constructive programs to take this country out of a disastrous crisis. Although the government has not been successful in solving the economic problems so far, no other propositions are being considered. A tendency to silence opposition, even when it does not represent an immediate threat to the powers that be, is evident. Its source is quite obvious, too. In the countries with long-lasting democratic traditions and an independent media system, silencing like that would be impossible. Here it works.

Until perestroika, the word *opposition* was not even mentioned in the domestic policy. Having allowed introduction of a multiparty system, Michail Gorbachev formally legalized opposition. But theory is one thing and practice is another. Gorbachev's media tried to silence Yeltsin, pretending for as long as they could that he did not exist. Yeltsin's press does the same to its political opponents.

Press Secretary of the Russian Christian Democratic Movement Michail Bolotovsky, discussing coverage of the opposition political forces by the mass media, called it "liberal censorship," "a sly game of the power with the press that is still obedient to it."[1] Having mentioned Gorbachev's costly neglect of opposition, he warned that Yeltsin is now making the same mistake. For as long as the powers will use the "switch off" button of the microphone both in the Parliament and in the press to silence opponents, "the leaders will place traps not for the opposition, but for themselves personally," he wrote.

THE MEDIA AND ECONOMIC REFORM: WHO OWNS, WHO CONTROLS?

Although the mass media were the first winner of perestroika in politics, in one sense they became the first victim of the changes in the economy.

Evaluating the situation as a whole from the point of view of market structure development, the most significant results have been achieved in the media that do not require large capital investment for their production, namely, print (production might be even easier, cheaper, and more affordable if desktop publishing equipment were available). We have the beginnings of what looks like a market with some of its attributes, such as commercial (not limited by the government) prices for newsprint, production, distribution, and the product itself.

But it is a very strange, distorted market: Whereas the media were formerly controlled by an ideological monopoly, now the emerging market is being controlled by government structures that still control monopolies in newsprint production, printing plant ownership and operation, distribution, and so on. Since they have no competitors, the state enterprises can raise prices as high as they like, justifying it by the fact that now the country is going to have a market economy. For instance, as soon as the supply of newsprint is lower than demand, this kind of a market works only for the producer not the consumer. And, of course, it works for the government structures. The same is true for newspaper production facilities.

The prospects for real privatizing of television (this is an obvious case) and the printed press in this country are really questionable so far. One can "found" a newspaper or a magazine, as the press law provides, but as long as one can't own the means of production and must depend for supplies on essentially one source, one's position as a publisher will be vulnerable.

In the totalitarian economy, all production was always centrally planned and all products were centrally distributed. The mass media were no exception. Since they were vitally important to the very existence of the system, control was more complex. The media were under the ideological control of the Communist party, which in this particular case also took over some economic functions that were usually performed by the government. The media were centrally financed, centrally supplied, centrally distributed. Nobody calculated the real expenses of what was considered "ideological production." If the party decided to launch a newspaper, it was provided with an office, printing facilities, and newsprint at very low prices.

By virtue of its unique position, the party bureaucracy directly supervised distribution of newsprint, though in the other branches of the economy supplies were always managed by the government.

As everywhere in our distorted economy, these prices had no correlation with expenses. A producer's deficiency was reimbursed by the state. The system of delivery that was also supervised by the ideological authorities distributed propaganda materials throughout the country at fixed low prices. The official newspapers and magazines were very cheap to create the largest possible audience, while the unofficial press was non-existent. Of course, there were some publications that made a profit, but it was absorbed by the party-government structures and the system as a whole was subsidized from the budget.

Ideology regulated the economy. As the country has never had enough newsprint and magazine paper to satisfy all its needs, paper supplies and corresponding circulation limits for every publication for the next year were dictated at the highest levels. But publications did not enjoy equal treatment. Judgments were made on a purely ideological basis. The Communist party and government publications had no limitations but the people could not subscribe to popular women's or literary magazines or a journal for motorists. Thus, the system of propaganda was regulated at its very foundation by distribution of paper. Anti-Communist publications were not allowed to be published at all. Even journals for pre-school kids had to be "ideologically restrained." Publications that directly promoted Communist ideology were given top priority.

It is no wonder that *Pravda* had the largest circulation in the country. The unlimited paper supply was one factor that accounted for it; Communist party discipline was the other. Subscription was organized in working places, and local party committees and cells strictly supervised the process, regularly reporting to the upper committee on how it was proceeding. The goal was to have the number of subscribers to the party publications as high as possible, and never lower than some specific number required by the upper party committee. Every Communist was obliged to subscribe either to a party newspaper or to a party magazine. Because of this system, the party publications had largest multimillion-reader circulations. Besides, all the most important information originated with the Party elite, so reading its publications was a must for anyone who tried to follow events.

Another factor of party dominance of the media field was the fact that its publishing houses controlled most of the printing facilities for newspapers and periodicals in the country. On one hand, this control made it possible for them to get profits from the publications they printed. On the other, the party used its ownership of the printing plants as one more instrument to influence the media.

After the Communist party was prohibited, the Russian government took over its facilities. Now it can use the profits from the publishing houses to subsidize its own publications. The Ministry of Press and Mass Information of Russia is now directly in charge of them. Party control over the printing presses has been replaced by state control. It is highly doubtful that this change will give more freedom to the Russian press.

Having seized the Pressa Publishing House (former Pravda Publishers), the government assumed control over the largest printing plant in the country where most of the national newspapers with the highest circulations are produced. The newspapers are fully dependent on this particular publisher because no other facility is powerful enough to produce millions of copies daily. Monopoly control of access to printing presses is a reliable substitute for the ideological monopoly the Communist party exercised in the past.

In some sense the situation of the smaller new publications that have low circulations is easier because they have some choice of printing facilities. But more than enough problems remain. Poignant efforts to reform the totalitarian economy were not successful. When the economy started failing, the press was among the first to suffer. Since the late 1980s production expenses have been growing rapidly, as have newsprint and distribution costs.

Newsprint production in the country is a government monopoly. A handful of paper mills supply all the press. All kinds of printing paper have always been in short supply. When the absolute monopoly of the Communist party of "ideological production" started to deteriorate, fixed prices on newsprint were lifted. The sharp increase in prices was formally justified by the "market economy." In fact it had nothing to do with the market: There was no competition of producers, and the price was not a result of supply and demand. Consumers had no voice at all, whereas the producers could charge monopoly prices. The government has been encouraging this kind of "market" and makes profits from it.

Newsprint problems are not limited to high prices. There are also severe paper shortages. As a result, newspapers cannot even fulfill their obligations to subscribers. Shortages were demonstrated in the most extreme form early in 1992, when one day *Soviet Byelorussia*, the major republican newspaper, published just one copy because of lack of paper. The copy was displayed in a window of the editorial office and attracted media attention throughout the country. But a failure to issue a newspaper because of newsprint shortages is by no means unique. A paper crisis in the Ukraine left the readers without newspapers for several days.

The rise in newsprint prices was the first big shock for the printed press in the time of perestroika; the second shock was the skyrocketing distribution rates. Here again the large national media were affected most because most of the new publications had local readership. As soon as the press distribution system Soyuzpechat was a government monopoly, too, it could dictate its terms to the newspapers and magazines.

After the Soviet Union disintegrated, Soyuzpechat split into a number of national systems, one in each of the new independent states. Every one of them has been enjoying the same monopoly. A few attempts to organize alternative delivery services could not really challenge this monopoly. In 1992 inflation speeded up the rise of distribution prices. Subscription prices announced in March 1993 for delivery in the second half of the year accounted two thirds of the total price, and a customer had to pay separately for the newspaper and for its delivery. Thus, the price of *Nezavisimaya gazeta*, as set by the publisher was 487 roubles, but to get it a subscriber had to pay a total of 1207 roubles. Other dailies are priced even higher. Contrary to worldwide practice, most newspapers and periodicals in Russia do not print their prices under the headline. Instead, they say: "Free price for newsstand sales." To illustrate the rate of inflation it is enough to note that until the early 1990s an annual subscription for a daily in the Soviet Union was around 10 roubles.

Another problem is that as soon as the state post offices control all subscription they have a potential to abuse this monopoly. At least, though, there were some customer complaints published stating that some post offices refused subscriptions to the opposition newspapers *Pravda* and *Sovetskaya Rossiya*.

Regardless of price, the postal system often fails to deliver publications on time, and may not deliver some issues at all.

Because of financial difficulties and hard currency shortages, the Soviet newspapers had to close their foreign bureaus. Of course, this did not improve the quality of coverage.

The entire deteriorating economy has been affecting newspaper production in the most disastrous way. It has caused breakdowns of electricity supplies, which have resulted in inability to produce newspapers, and gas shortages, which have frustrated distribution.

In the huge territory of Russia, where national newspapers have traditionally been distributed throughout the entire country, failures in the normal working of railroads and air transportation have become rather common. This means that readers often get today's newspaper tomorrow or even later, resulting in smaller readership and harm to the market generally.

Increasing publishing and distribution costs have brought about jumps in subscription and newsstand prices. Circulation decreases have further complicated conditions for the press. Circulations are falling as a result of growing prices, rapidly widening choices for the reader, and people's changing preferences. In 1991 the Soviet press lost one third of its 1990 subscribers, even though numerous new publications were started.

The trend has continued. According to the results of subscription for 1993, *Izvestiya* has kept 25% of the 1992 subscribers (800,000 compared to 3,200,000), *Komsomolskaya pravda*—15% (1,831,000 of 12,941,000), *Nezavisimaya gazeta*—39% (27,000 of 70,000), a weekly *Argumenti i facti*—35% (8,873,000 of 25,693,000).

Conservative papers, though their circulations are lower, lost a smaller percentage of their readership than those considered democratic: *Pravda* preserved 49% (479,000 of 983,000), *Sovetskaya Rossiya*—48% (407,000 of 850,000). There may be a number of reasons for this trend, but failure of efforts by Yeltsin's government to reform the economy is evidently number one. The newspaper that performed best of all was *Rossiiskaya gazeta*, started by the Supreme Soviet of Russia in 1990. It kept 94% of its subscribers (632,000 of 677,000).

The only newspaper that gained circulation as a result of the subscription campaign for 1993 was a weekly, *Moscow news* (from 367,000 to 485,000). There were speculations in *Pravda* that the paper reached this result, contradicting the general trend, by distributing free subscriptions though the reason for this charity is unknown.

Argumenti i fakti conducted a survey to find out why its subscription rate had declined by an analysis of 936 letters to the editor. Of the respondents 346 stated that increased cost was the main reason for their refusal to subscribe. In 140 cases, the post office refused applications for subscription; another 120 readers had lost interest in the press in general because glasnost had failed to solve the country's major problems.[2]

Bankruptcies of newspapers and periodicals in this highly unfavorable economic environment are inevitable. In fact, some have already suspended publication. It is an obvious loss for their readers, of course. It is also a very serious threat to journalists who face unemployment.

At the end of 1992 even the largest newspapers were in the red. The debt of *Komsomolskaya pravda* to Pressa publishing house was 51 million roubles; *Pravda*'s, about 15 million; *Sovetskaya Rossiya*'s, over 6 million. At the same time the debt of Pressa itself was 200 million, and it threatened to stop printing these newspapers. Thanks to government subsidies the problem was solved, and the papers continued publication.

The first thing the press is doing to improve its financial situation is publishing advertising. It is a rather new phenomenon for this country. Until the late 1980s, only local newspapers published a limited number of classifieds and commercial advertisements. Growing expenses made all the press look for the new sources of income.

Weakening of party control was another important factor that promoted development of advertising because ideological purists on the very top had always rejected "commercialization of the press" in principle. It may seem that a reason for this was an unwillingness to share influence but in a totalitarian society with centralized control over everything that was not the problem. Basically advertising was rejected because the media were tools of ideology and propaganda and commercial ads did not fit in with this concept. Local newspapers with small budgets were allowed to print ads but national papers, which dominated the media scene and served as windows to the system, were not.

Political and ideological advertising was widely used. Slogans like "Long live the Communist Party" or "Let us fulfill the five-year plan ahead of time" surrounded people everywhere. But this is not the kind of advertising that brings in money. In a planned system with its totally controlled production and distribution, there is not much need for the promotion of goods as in market economies. Hence, we have not developed print advertising very far.

The most important problem now is a lack of consumer advertising caused by the collapse of the consumer market: there are no products to sell and nothing to advertise. Producers don't compete for consumers; buyers compete for goods.

Nevertheless, newspapers publish enough ads, sometimes up to 50 percent of their space; and this progress is too rapid for publications that two or three years ago did not have a single commercial line. The general-interest newspapers of four to eight pages are filled with the kind of ads that are published in the business section of *The New York Times* or trade publications. These are mostly advertisements of commercial (non-government) banks, companies, and exchanges, not consumer advertising. They have money to spend and know that they are supposed to advertise but have a very vague idea of what exactly their target audiences should be and where they should invest to reach them.

These commercial entities are newcomers in the economy and have very limited business experience. It will take them time to learn some basic facts about marketing and advertising strategies and find out that general interest newspapers are normally used to advertise consumer goods. But on the other hand, it will also take time to develop a system of trade publications that will better serve their purposes. It is an integral part of a normal market economy, but does not exist in this country.

A negative secondary result of commercialization is the corruption of the press. The public is not aware of it yet but it is already widespread. Concealed commercials are presented as regular reports or interviews. Journalists write them for bribes.

To increase advertising revenues, newspaper managers use swindling. As a news program on the Russian TV "Vesti" reported on December 17, 1991, a substantial part of the circulation of the business daily *Delovoi mir* is not even delivered to newsstands, but goes directly to recycling.

The news in *Delovoi mir* is minimal: just four pages compared to twelve pages of advertising. The newspaper's advertising rates are among the highest. There can be only one reason for printing tens of thousands of copies that never get to the reader and are immediately recycled: to support advertising rates at a high level.

Early in 1992, a number of new businesses formed the Russian Advertisers Association. It is designed to protect their interests and regulate their relationships with the mass media. The association also intends to improve the quality of advertising. It plans to introduce to the Supreme Soviet a draft law on advertising or special amendments to the press law.

Newspapers and magazines have other means than advertising for increasing their budgets. They diversify their activities: launch supplements and separate publications, produce videos based on their materials, organize advertising companies, poll public opinion, and enter into joint ventures with the other mass media and foreign companies. This kind of diversification of business activities is quite a new phenomenon for this country and it was made possible by perestroika.

Economic problems of the audiovisual media are easier to describe because the system is entirely state controlled. The major change is the disappearance of what used to be Gosteleradio and later the All-Union TV and Radio Company caused by the collapse of the Union. It creates more democracy only in the sense that control has been shifted to the level of the former republics, the present sovereign states. But each still does the same state TV and radio broadcasting, financed from the budget.

In the Union system the major expense of the central TV was not programming, but transmission costs. It took about two thirds of the budget to cover the huge territory of the country: satellites, transmitters, receivers, and their operation. The Ministry of Communications was in charge of the entire system and so this part of the national TV budget was reallocated directly to it.

There is some ambiguity in the present role of the former central TV (now the Ostankino company). The Russian government took it over and started financing it. Meanwhile, the Commonwealth of Independent States (CIS) decided that the channel should serve all of them and provide a "common information space." But no concrete organizational or financial measures were taken to realize this idea.

Above all, some republics have already announced that they have no money to pay for retransmissions of the channel on their territories; others have decided to use this particular frequency for their own broadcasting. It does not seem possible now that the CIS members will be able to agree on this matter and develop the channel as a joint venture.

The financial problems of television were worsened by a demand of the Goskino (State Committee on Cinematography) to pay for the movies shown on TV, something that was never done before. In the new economic conditions, the moviemakers started counting their revenues and losses and decided not to provide their productions free any longer. The situation for sports events and entertainment is the same.

Shortages of electricity have caused interruptions of TV broadcasting in different regions of the country for days and sometimes weeks.

Expansion of commercials on TV has been speedier and even less attractive than in the press. That is natural because much more money was invested there. Problems of advertising on TV are basically like those in the press. But one is especially vital in TV: quality. On TV much more expertise is needed than in the printed media, where text ads have been predominant so far. Lack of professionalism, low ethical standards, and poor taste cannot produce good commercials.

But advertisers bring profits and as soon as really big money is involved here, in an ethical vacuum, they corrupt this medium even more than the press. It is not only interviews or reports that represent advertising not identified as such but entire programs. As in the cases of hidden advertising in the press, those programs usually cover the alternative economic structures. They are paid for either legally, to the company, or illegally, directly to the TV team. The method of payment does not make much difference to a TV viewer, who is deceived in both cases.

The phenomenon of widespread bribery on national TV has been publicly recognized by the chairman of the All-Russian TV and Radio Company Ostankino (formerly All-Union TV and Radio) Yegor Yakovlev, who has said that "the level of corruption around advertising, including information programs, is difficult to describe."[3] But this open statement has not led to any positive changes.

I see the major reason as the fact that the gold mine of TV, although it has controllers, supervisors, and gatekeepers, does not have a real owner. The state has been highly efficient in exploiting TV as an instrument of Communist politics, propaganda, and ideology. But it long ago proved a failure in management of the economy, and now, when the TV company is facing new economic realities, its directors are unable to handle the problems.

Of course, the journalists' ethics (or in this case, their lack) is highly important in this respect, too. But the wide scope of corruption leads us to suppose that the system itself is breeding bribery by allowing or probably even encouraging it.

We live in a society that has never been governed by law and has entirely rejected the very notion of private ownership. Everything used to belong to the state or to the Communist party on top of it. Formally state property was considered "the people's property," or, in other words, nobody's property. But in fact, it was governed by the ruling elite for its own benefit. Now, with the Union ruined and the party gone, this uncertainty of ownership creates problems.

The first press law in our history cleverly avoids any mention of ownership. But we have had a lot of cases where journalists declared themselves "founders" (a term introduced by the press law) of long existing publications and were issued registration certificates that validate that claim. The absence, in the existing law, of the very notion of an owner of a mass medium reflects an old Communist dogma that owners and "the control of the capital" exist *there*, in the West, but *here* the press belongs to the people and reflects their interests. The term *founder* was evidently introduced to avoid the ideologically sensitive question of who owns the media. This tribute to the past does not help the democratic restructuring of the mass media. On the contrary, it creates opportunities for abuses of media power.

In 1917, the Bolsheviks moved forward with slogans: "Land to the peasants, factories to the workers" (although no such promise was really fulfilled). In the period of perestroika people who considered themselves democrats added "Newspapers to the journalists." In the conditions of the collapsing Communist power, this slogan worked in quite a number of cases. An "editorial collective" emerges as a "founder," as the law says, of a mass medium. In fact, it looks more like expropriation, reproducing the old mode of behavior of the Bolsheviks after the 1917 revolution when they called upon the lumpen society to "rob what has been robbed." The logic of the journalists is quite simple: we make the newspaper; that means we have all the right to be its "founders."

It appears that the lesson of the destructive experience of collectivization of farming has not been learned. "Collective newspapers" are not much different, just another variant of the old Communist myth. Typically, the journalists involved do not even consider themselves owners, just founders. The economic organization of the mass media cannot be changed by the these means.

The Russian government in the post-Gorbachev period has not taken further steps to promote the development of the independent media. On the contrary, it has confirmed its tendency to statification of the media by a number of measures: immediately taking over the propaganda structures of the former Union; launching and supporting from the state budget its own newspapers and periodicals, which enjoy "the most favorable media" stature in the pressing and competitive economic environment; merging the two news agencies, TASS and RIAN, into one information monopoly under government control, and directly prohibiting privatization of TV, radio, and the communications infrastructure. The state keeps exercising its ownership right to preserve its control of public opinion.

Real freedom of the press, not just glasnost, will develop in this country only when new political forces that can provide a real alternative to government power emerge. This will happen when a genuine civil society is formed. Establishing a new class of owners will be the first step. So far it has been a lumpen society, where the social foundations of the present power and opposition are rather vaguely determined. This vagueness can be a source of instability, leading to a destruction of the political balance.

THE MEDIA AND A TREND TO SEPARATISM: ADDING FUEL TO THE FIRE OF CONFLICT

The national movements throughout the Soviet Union brought about a breakup of the nation into a number of sovereign states. The Baltic republics were the first to restore the independence they'd had before they were annexed on the eve of the World War II. The chain reaction could not be stopped. As a result, countries that for centuries had been a part of the Russian Empire—the Ukraine, Byelorussia, the Caucasian and Central Asian republics—have all seceded, too.

Reasons for the rise of the ethnic movements throughout the country were quite objective and very strong. The national identities of the numerous peoples inhabiting the Soviet Union had been ignored for the sake of the "new historical commonality—the Soviet people." National problems and conflicts were silenced, concealed, and suppressed. The pressure of the system was perceived by many people, especially non-Russians, as national pressure. The ideological and political dictatorship was blamed mostly on the "Center," that is, the Moscow authorities, often identified with the Russians.

Whereas in Russia the relaxation of ideological pressure from the beginning gave rise to democratic trends (as well as other suppressed ideologies, of course), in the other republics, it stimulated nationalism first and foremost.

On the other hand, this objective tendency was skillfully used by the authorities in most of the republics. They offered the people the idea of the nation as a substitute for Communist ideology at the moment when the rejection of Communism by the public was widespread. Under this new banner, the republican leaders—former Communist nomenklatura—intended to achieve their own political and personal goals, namely, to preserve their power and conserve the old system in one form or another.

National movements were often inimical to among the ideal of a free press as well. In Uzbekistan the authorities reportedly forbade local media to report the riots in Namangan and residents of the republic have learned about them only from the central press and TV. When journalists visited Namangan from the other republics or from abroad, their activities were strictly controlled. There were cases of confiscation of notebooks and tapes. A number of journalists were just expelled. In Turkmenia the local journalists could not get critical articles published.

And the republican government censors more than just local media. A part of circulation of the central newspapers that is to be distributed in Uzbekistan and border regions of Kazakhstan and Turkmenia is printed in Tashkent. Before printing the newspapers local censors check them to take out criticism of the republican authorities and put in other materials. An issue of *Izvestiya* (Number 247, 1992) that contained a direct appeal to the president of the republic Karimov to stop censorship was not printed at all. 155,000 copies of the newspaper were removed from circulation. Political censorship went as far as prohibiting subscription in the republic to *Izvestiya*, *Komsomolskaya pravda*, and *Argimenti i facti* for 1993. Moldavian authorities did the same.

In the Ukraine, a newspaper published by the national movement Rukh, *Narodna hazeta*, stopped appearing because of a bureaucratic conspiracy to block supplies of paper and printing equipment. Although the paper was legally registered and had eighty-six thousand subscribers, the paper's deputy editor charged, that, among other difficulties, the Communist party handed down orders to Kiev printing plants to bar *Narodna hazeta* access to their services.

In Byelorussia, the Communist party also tried to control democratic publications, even those were published by official organizations. The Communist nomenklatura stepped forward against *Narodna hazeta*, a newspaper of the republican Supreme Soviet that strove to present the viewpoints of all deputies, both the conservatives and the non-Communist opposition. A leader of the Byelorussian Communist party, Anatoly Malofeev, called upon Communist deputies to interfere in the affairs of the newspaper. He demanded an end to the access of "various dubious newspapers" to the printing facilities of the Communist party.

The Ukrainian president, Leonid Kravchuk, used to be the top Communist ideologist in the republic. The president of Tajikistan, Rakhmon Nabijev, was the leader of the republican Communist party. The heads of the other Central Asian republics belonged to the party elite, too, as was Aiaz Mutalibov, the president of Azerbaijan. All those apparatchiks exploited their people's aspirations for freedom and sovereignty and gained power under the banner of national independence. They won their personal fight for power but there is still the question of what their nations gained, if anything.

The situation in the Baltics was different from that in most of the regions of the former USSR. One reason is that the period of the Communist rule there was much shorter than everywhere else. But what is probably still more important is that those countries already had democratic political traditions which were interrupted by the Soviet invasion in 1940. In the Russian Empire, as well as in the Soviet Union that became its successor, democracy was never known. It is no wonder that the Baltic countries were the first and the most determined fighters for independence: they sought to restore both the national sovereignty and the democracy that the people had not forgotten.

The Union authorities have been struggling for a long time to keep all the republics together while the latter have been pressing for secession and neither side has felt like compromising. At the beginning, the forces were absolutely unequal. But Michail Gorbachev's rejection of totalitarian ideology and totalitarian politics strictly limited the methods the Center could use in this struggle.

Unfortunately, there were several tragedies when the military forces were used against civilians in sharp contradiction of Gorbachev's "new thinking." But it is an achievement of perestroika that direct violence against people was no longer considered an acceptable instrument of domestic politics. Otherwise, the course of the developments in the last few years would have been quite different.

All the republics of the Union followed the example of the Baltics, although on somewhat different grounds. The motto "National Independence" was the same everywhere. But in a number of cases sovereignty was declared not to promote democracy but to stop Gorbachev's policy of reforms at the border of a republic.

On the other hand, the central government by its tough opposition (at the first stage, it was actually complete rejection) to the ethnic movements, regardless of their nature, further stimulated nationalism and gave the republican leaders more arguments to support their resistance to the Center in public opinion. The uncompromising position taken by both sides brought about a clash that radicalized the national movements.

The conflict between the Center and the republics turned into a media war because the mainstream press and TV were government controlled on both sides. And both sides did their best to redouble troubles and conflicts instead of looking for common ground and trying to compromise. The "media war" was seen not only in the content of articles and TV reports but in the attempts by local authorities to close local bureaus of the central media in the republics and expel correspondents. In some cases distribution of All-Union newspapers was prevented and central TV broadcasts were switched off. Public opinion supported this policy, too. Demonstrations in the capitals of the republics against central media misinformation about republican issues demanded it.

The All-Union media did their part in the suppression: by expressing prevailing biases, by providing propaganda justification of military actions, by misrepresenting the real reasons for republican actions, and by silencing their results. One of the broadest propaganda campaigns of the last period of the USSR was organized to prevent the disintegration of the Union on the eve of the referendum to decide its future. One of the secret instructions issued by the Moscow City Communist Party Committee to lower party organizations before the referendum advised against appealing to the voter's mind because this approach was considered good only in dealing with the intelligentsia. There was an order to aim for "direct stimulation of the desired behavior" by high-pressure propaganda that "stresses one option to the exclusion of all others." Propaganda, the instruction said, must be "as massive as possible," filling every available channel of the mass media. Recommended slogans included a baby crying "Mummy! Safeguard my future! Vote 'yes'! "[4]

The Soviet media coverage of the long-lasting and the bloody Armenian-Azerbaijani conflict in Nagorni Karabakh was misleading from the very beginning. TASS reported only incidents in which Armenia seemed to be the aggressor. The central government in effect supported the more conservative and yielding Azerbaijanian authorities against nationalist Armenian leadership seeking independence. Besides, the Supreme Soviet of Armenia nationalized Communist party property and declared all the party and Comsomol assets in the republic to be state owned on the grounds that the party's wealth was created at the expense of the state.

The Central Committee of the Communist Party of the Soviet Union protested the resolution.

At one of his press conferences the chairman of Gosteleradio, Leonid Kravchenko, confirmed that the Soviet media had deliberately distorted coverage of the ongoing interethnic conflict in Nagorni Karabakh to give the impression that casualties on both sides were more or less equal. Both Armenia and Azerbaijan have accused the Soviet media of lacking objectivity in reporting the situation in Karabakh.[5]

Intolerance of different opinions and inability to conceive opposition without hostility, cultivated in the people by the Communist ideologists, were manifested by both sides. The national conflicts were not resolved but, on the contrary, became more acute. The mass media's contribution to the problem was quite substantial. Dependence and habitual obedience made them submissive instruments of politicians.

Misinformation campaigns in the mainstream Soviet media were widely used against ethnic movements. One of the most extensive was that against Lithuania. It started in March 1990, when the republic, the first in the Soviet Union, declared its independence. All efforts were taken to prevent its secession. "The campaign appears to be unprecedented in the era of glasnost and can only be compared with the Soviet media coverage of the Soviet invasion of Czechoslovakia in 1968."[6]

Propaganda campaigns were organized to justify bloodshed in Tbilisi, crackdowns in Lithuania and Latvia, and other tragic episodes. The official propaganda did its best to censor information in such a way that it would be close to impossible to understand what was really going on from outside a republic. In April 1989, when a demonstration of civilians was crushed by the military in Tbilisi, this propaganda campaign was more or less successful, at least at the beginning, and dissident voices could hardly by heard. But in January 1991, after the crackdown in Lithuania, the government failed to manipulate a number of the national media and they spoke out against the military action.

Outraged, Michail Gorbachev encouraged the Parliament to suspend the press law because "we need objectivity." In fact he pleaded for reinstating censorship. At a closed session of the Supreme Soviet of the USSR he suggested that the Press Law that eliminated censorship should be abolished "for the time being." Gorbachev cited *Moscow news*, which blamed him for the "grave crime" committed in Lithuania. (This edition of the newspaper seems to have been confiscated by the authorities, which is itself illegal.) The suggestion was rejected by liberal deputies.[7]

The Soviet leadership had already had a very impressive and productive experience of "temporary" suspension of freedom of the press in 1918: the "time being" was more than seventy years.

By making his proposal Michail Gorbachev demonstrated again that glasnost is not the equivalent of freedom of the press. The president proposed the formation of a parliamentary committee to ensure "objectivity" in news coverage—in effect restoring the censorship abolished by the press law. It did not work but the president's action was typical of a Communist leader. Looking back, it is really unimaginable how Gorbachev, raised and promoted by the Communist system, managed to challenge so many of its assumptions and began to reform it.

It's interesting that Gorbachev's proposal to reinstate censorship was censored by the official media. Neither the first channel of the central TV, that had covered practically all the territory of the Soviet Union, nor its second channel, that had a smaller audience and fewer broadcasting hours mentioned Gorbachev's proposal to suspend the Law on the Press. Also unreported were critical remarks by many deputies on the performance of Soviet TV under Leonid Kravchenko.

The Soviet media were also silent about support of the Balts in the other republics. Neither radio nor TV nor official news agencies informed the public that the Ukrainian, Byelorussian, and Kazakh Supreme Soviets condemned the use of force in Lithuania. Because of this, Yeltsin and the Supreme Soviet of Russia, whose opposition could not be silenced, looked like the lone dissenting voices in the government.

In Estonia, although Moscow managed to do without using troops, but it supported the anti-secession forces, the so-called Intermovement, by other means. The military authorities stationed in the republic installed powerful radio and TV transmitters, which were partly intended to serve the military but mainly to reinforce the system of central propaganda. The first channel of the central TV was given one more frequency so it could broadcast over a larger area.

The stations that spoke against the Estonian government were located on the premises of the Soviet military units in Tallinn, the capital of the republic. Nadezhda (Hope)—the name of both TV and radio stations—broadcasted in support of Intermovement. The local authorities were not asked for permission either to build the transmitters or to go on the air. Everything was decided, organized, and funded by the Union powers. The stations were registered by the All-Union State TV and Radio Company although their broadcasting range was limited by the republican borders and according to the rules it was the Estonian government that had to authorize broadcasting in its territory.

The radio station Nadezhda called on listeners to form paramilitary units in opposition to Estonian independence.

TV Nadezhda was launched in spring 1991, when the Russian government was still fighting against the Center. It tried to get equipment and technology for its own TV broadcasting but was constantly denied.

Several months earlier, in February, Russian radio was banned from using the frequencies of the first and the second All-Union radio channels, which covered all the territory of the USSR. Instead, it had to use the third channel, which had a narrower range. The restrictions were reportedly imposed after Gorbachev complained to Kravchenko about Radio Rossiya's coverage of the events in the Baltics. As a result, the audience of Radio Rossiya was cut by over a third: only 60 percent of the population of Russia was able to listen to it. The general director of radio broadcasting of the All-Union TV and Radio Company, Anatoly Tupikin, warned the republican authorities that if the Russian radio continued its criticism of the USSR leadership, it would be taken off the air entirely. In response, the Russian government decided to establish its own radio structure, withdrawing the necessary amount of money to finance it (4 billion rubles) from the contribution of the RSFSR to the All-Union budget.[8]

The Ukrainian authorities blamed the Union officials for the biased coverage of events in the republic by their media, especially TV. On the eve of the Ukrainian referendum on independence, the leader of the republic, Leonid Kravchuk, demanded time on central TV. He stressed that public opinion perceived that kind of coverage as inflaming an anti-Ukrainian mood and as attempting to provoke Ukraine and Russia into a quarrel. The presentation was broadcast, but the TV officials could not refrain from commenting on it in a manner that, in the Ukrainian republic was considered disrespectful to the head of the state.[9]

The Soviet habit of total control over information and propaganda activities is strong. Both camouflaged Communists and open anti-Communists continue to practice it. The short presidency of Zviad Gamsakhurdia in Georgia is probably the most astonishing demonstration of how strong and deeply rooted the Communist mentality is. Having come to power, the dissident, a political opponent of the system, started behaving like an insider.

Actually the Georgian opposition had deprived the republican Communist party of access to the media even before Gamsakhurdia came to power. Within a month before the elections in October 1990 the Georgian Supreme Soviet confiscated all printing equipment owned by the Communists and took over both the Georgian and the Russian language daily newspapers.

"The power that does not recognize the opposition can not be called power," Gamsakhurdia liked to repeat, when he was an opponent of the government.[10] Nevertheless, when he was elected president, his mode of action was not that of a democratic but an authoritarian leader. He treated the mass media exactly as his Communist predecessors had. He organized an entire propaganda network of his own. He banned TV broadcasts from Moscow because of the criticism they contained. In his last six months in power, he dismissed five editors of Georgian newspapers that published materials critical of him and his presidency. In reality the national idea as he practiced it turned out to be pretty much like totalitarianism.

The victory of the democratic forces of Russia headed by President Yeltsin against the Communist plotters in August 1991 sped up the centrifugal trends. It is not just the Communist party that has been defeated, but the central power structures as a whole. Although not all of them were immediately dissolved, the process has started and the December statement by the heads of Russia, Ukraine, and Byelorussia about disintegration of the Union and formation of the Commonwealth of Independent States has only formalized matters.

To the Center, whether it was good or bad, all of the republics were equal. After the collapse of the Union the smaller republics found themselves vis-à-vis huge Russia and its unpredictable leader. Although formally the Center still existed, Gorbachev in fact had all the power. The reaction of all the republics was the same: they rushed to escape by formalizing their sovereign stature.

The national idea brought about a breakup of the Soviet Union into a number of sovereign states. But it did not and could not automatically give them freedom and democracy. The fact is that most of those states are just replicas of the old Union and they have inherited its totalitarian traditions. Now each will have to solve its own problems and the old problems remain.

For as long as the state is able to control or influence the mass media, either through politics or economics, there is always potential for manipulation. It would be naive to believe that the governments of the new states will wish or will be able to pursue the politics of destatization in the sphere of the press. In the Soviet Union, ideology has always been considered one of the most significant fields of government activity and control. The present generation of politicians will hardly be able to break this tradition. And they definitely will be unable to do so soon.

FREEDOM AS A STATE OF MIND

The idea of freedom as a natural human right ("all people are born free") is quite new to this country, or at least to the overwhelming majority of its population. In the course of its history, it has never experienced freedom. After centuries of being obedient subjects of the "Tsar-Father" people found themselves under the control of a still more dominant totalitarian regime. It was violent and repressive, but at the same time unbelievably hypocritical. After depriving its citizens of practically all freedoms, the state promised them "a kingdom of freedom" in a distant Communist future.

As to the fate of living generations, they were supposed to sacrifice for the sake of this future. The official ideology never admitted openly that people had been deprived of their natural human rights. The rulers of the country would probably have preferred to ignore the very notion of freedom but, as long as that was impossible, they interpreted it in a really ridiculous, Orwellian way.

Several generations of people in this country grew up under the pressure of the Marxist interpretation of freedom as "a realized necessity." All the textbooks on Marxism (and practically everyone from schoolchildren to nurses to engineers had to study it in one form or another) taught that one cannot live in a society and also be free. This implied that individual freedoms must be immolated for the sake of the state.

A concept of a state as the highest priority of all the people and individual human rights as something meaningless and inferior was at the core of the totalitarian ideology. The might and prosperity of the state were supposed to be the highest personal values for everyone and trust in this myth was considered by the official ideology an equivalent of freedom.

After 1985, restrictions of individual freedoms set up by the Communist party and the state started growing weaker and vanishing. Although we are far from having all the freedoms people in the Western democracies have been enjoying for centuries, we are still moving in the right direction.

But by now it has become evident that the ongoing process of liberation is, although important, the easier part of the job we have to do. Having removed a number of external restrictions, we suddenly realize that our internal restrictions are even more powerful and are much more difficult to leave behind.

Until recently, in this country freedom was perceived as an abstract notion. Now, when it is slowly emerging as a reality, most people do not know what it is or how to handle it. What does it mean to be free for an individual and a society? Are we ready to be free? Do we need to be free? What is the price of freedom? Are we prepared to pay it? There are lots of questions and not so many answers. Nowadays in the former Soviet Union, those questions are not so purely philosophical as they used to be but quite practical.

In this country with its heavy totalitarian heritage, the most basic understanding of freedom is freedom from fear—of being arrested, repressed, humiliated, and otherwise abused by the all-powerful and uncontrolled authorities. The first rule of survival in this unequal fight of the individual against the state has been never to reveal lack of loyalty—it was too dangerous. In those rare cases when somebody dared to exercise freedom of speech or of the press (both were proclaimed by the Constitution), personal freedom could be at stake.

At the same time, suppression by the system was so constant and long lasting that people generally accepted it as a given and barely recognized it in their everyday lives. Dependence of the individual on the state was global: Only the state could employ people. Only the state could house them. Only the state could educate them. And so on. People had no choice but to be loyal; otherwise they would be thrown out of the society.

This loyalty extended to Communist doctrine, too, not because people were convinced believers but because they had no choice: it was reality and the majority hardly ever thought of it.

On the other hand, the Communist ideology, although it may seem to have passed through people's minds barely acknowledged, cultivated intolerance. It did so by excluding all doubts, all variations, all alternatives. And among the masses it was not intolerance to the opponent of what was called "the only right theory," which people did not really care about anyway. It was a much broader intolerance, to everything different, strange, or non-conformist.

Such thinking was the result of several generations of brainwashing, of course. But it must also have arisen from the memories of terror that are deep in the genes of people in this country. There are memories about repressions against countrymen, sometimes family members, who were somehow different from the others in their views or were just accused of being different. There was rather a long period in Soviet history when being different was more than enough justification for being imprisoned or even executed.

The policy of glasnost essentially implied that people and the news media were allowed to say what they thought without fear of repression. That does not mean that all the limitations and taboos collapsed overnight. The process has been long and painful, marked not only by advances but by retreats. Nevertheless, the result in this particular area is amazing. Though the authorities keep trying to tame the media, pluralism has emerged versus dominant ideology.

The free market of ideas in this country has been developing much more rapidly than that of the economy. The significance of this development cannot be overestimated. But at the same time the process has revealed some flaws that the society has not been ready to face. What is worse, many media professionals seem not to recognize those problems at all or prefer not to see them.

The advantages of the new media market are obvious, particularly in the printed press: diversification of media voices, multiplicity of views, and plurality of opinions. There are some new radio stations on the air. Changes in TV are least noticeable, primarily because of the dominance of two monopolies: the state television and radio which controls virtually all programming, and the Ministry of Communications, which is in charge of the whole telecommunications infrastructure in the country.

Regardless of the good intentions declared by state officials, the strong and long-lasting tradition of authoritarian leadership in this country dispels any illusion that the tremendous power of the state controlled mass media will always be used by officials for the benefit of the whole society.

On the other hand, the most important journalistic tradition that several generations of media professionals in this country have been taught to promote is support of the powers that be. It is not a question of ideological convictions or moral principles, just a question of survival.

Ideological control extended to the very basis of the profession—the system of journalism education. There were only about two dozen schools for the whole country. To be accepted, one had to be recommended by a Comsomol or a Communist party committee.

Journalism craft in the curriculum was secondary to Communist indoctrination—Marxist philosophy, political economy, history of the Communist party and its press. All the general subjects, such as literature and history, were presented from the Marxist-Leninist point of view, too.

Students have never been taught to separate news from opinion. On the contrary, they have been persuaded that information is a kind of a propaganda too and should be properly interpreted and commented on so that people can understand it correctly (from the standpoint of the Communist doctrine). The situation was compounded by the fact that until most recently the notion of journalism ethics was unknown in this country; it was neither studied nor practiced. Party-mindedness and class interests were the chief principles that guided journalists' everyday work and justified everything.

Actually, these were not professional schools but, as their administrators proudly described them to the students, "ideological schools." Proudly, because ideology was a sacred Party domain. No dissent, no criticism, no doubt about the Communist doctrine was allowed in the journalism schools. Nobody really cared what students thought, but they were supposed to say and write what was expected. Those who dared to violate the rule were immediately expelled and the others received a very convincing lesson. Students were supposed to become "the Party journalists"—or not become journalists at all.

It would have been easier to submit to it if it were a matter of sincere trust but it was not. Actually long before perestroika, the whole ideological machine was morally and intellectually depraved and so was the entire power system. It was not difficult to change convictions because in most cases there were no convictions at all. It was just a job of promoting definite ideas and defending definite causes. These ideas and causes were determined at the very top and orders were fully obeyed even if today they opposed the dicta of yesterday. As a result, the main lesson students learned was cynicism.

After this kind of education, or, more precisely, indoctrination, by the time of graduation, the future media professionals knew for sure that independence, opposition views, and a critical approach would not advance a career in journalism. On the contrary, they would probably ruin it. Conformity and loyalty provided the most reliable foundation for a career in journalism.

Glasnost has changed the system of values in the journalism profession. Within the last several years, quite a number of careers were built by opposition journalists. But the problem was that most of them continued to associate themselves directly with political forces as their predecessors had for several generations. Yes, this new breed of journalists spoke against the old authorities but they did so not as independent media professionals but as proponents of different groups and platforms.

Some television personalities became well known in the first period of liberalization of national TV but later disappeared when the politics of the country leadership and correspondingly of the TV establishment became tougher. They returned after the failed coup in August 1991. But now, when you watch them on the evening news, it sometimes appears that nothing has changed.

They support a definite political line as their forerunners did and do it with equal openness and enthusiasm. The difference is that this new generation looks more sincere. They supported the opposition and now that it has come to power, they are ready to serve it with their craft. Conformity seems to prevail forever.

Can journalists in a democratic society openly associate themselves with any political power without raising doubts about their professional integrity and trustworthiness? To TV viewers personal preferences of media people make no difference. The audience does not need to know them or to have opinion presented as unbiased reporting. People do not want to be taught what is good and what is bad, in the manner of Communist propaganda, and can decide for themselves when they are given accurate information.

But obtaining information as such is still a problem. It seems that the propaganda tradition in the media won't die. The difference is that some media people feel engaged by Communists, others by democrats (although this notion can be interpreted in different ways) or somebody else. For decades, journalists in this country have been taught in theory and in practice to serve as a voice for the authorities and they continue to do so; only the authorities have changed.

This is probably the key internal problem of the news media in this country that will determine their future: Will they prefer to be engaged or independent? To lend their pens to politicians or to inform the general public? An old tradition that is still very powerful here dictates the propaganda style but the vital interests of the society demand objectivity and impartial information.

It appears that journalists as a whole do not recognize this problem. They mistake liberation of the control of Communist nomenklatura for freedom. But in most cases it is just changing a gatekeeper: the one everybody is sick of for a new one who seems to be liberal and understanding.

The journalists became accustomed to being "underlings of the Party," as Nikita Khrushchev called them and that became a way of life. They have not recognized yet that they are (or can be) a power of their own—the fourth branch of government. In the past journalists could survive and prosper only if they identified themselves with the ruling powers. And this inclination to identification with a governing political group is still overwhelming although in so many other respects the situation in the country has changed.

Reasons for this kind of a conduct are also deeply rooted in the mass consciousness. Individualism has always been rejected by the official ideology. A person had no intrinsic value except as an integral part of a collective, a community, or an organization. And journalists were susceptible to all the pressure of this common assumption, too. And besides, they supported and developed this idea as propaganda specialists.

Equally important, journalists (like people here in general, of course) got used to seeing and interpreting the world from the standpoint of only one idea. Now it may be a different idea but journalists still feel commissioned to construe events from a given angle.

The deep personal and professional involvement of journalists in politics led to the election of some of them to the Union and republican legislatures. It was perceived both by the journalists and by the public as a victory for democracy. And while they keep sitting on two chairs, being both journalists and parliamentarians, neither the press nor the public can see the ethical problem, a conflict of interests though it is absolutely evident from a democratic viewpoint.

Another side of the problem of journalists' full dependence on the authorities is the problem of professionalism. For decades, ideological purity was considered a number one priority for a media person; all the other criteria were secondary. This means that the journalism craft itself was not greatly valued. Naturally this attitude resulted in low professional standards among the mass media, who were intended to satisfy the ideological bosses not the audiences.

Underestimation of professionalism also deprived a journalist of professional and personal freedom. He or she was not a respected specialist (a status that promotes personal independence) but a laborer with no value outside the power system. When Michail Nenashev was criticized for putting non-professionals in management roles in Gosteleradio, he responded that to be oriented only to professionalism is undemocratic.[11]

Total media dependence on the state made it easy for the KGB to recruit journalists. Secret services do it everywhere but in a totalitarian society, media people are especially vulnerable. The KGB infiltrated all the national media. There is an old story in the folklore of Moscow journalists about a foreign correspondent of *Komsomolskaya pravda*. He confused two channels of communication and as a result his newspaper received information about maneuvers of NATO troops, and the KGB got news about a zoo. This tale sounds apocryphal but it is true. And although the old KGB does not formally exist now, this is not merely a matter of the past.

A department of political information of the Novosti press agency was fully staffed with officers of the First Administration of the KGB; there were fifty of them.[12] When Yegor Yakovlev was appointed chairman of the All-Union State TV and Radio Company, one of the first things he did was to ask his counterpart at the KGB to call off his numerous officers who were working within the broadcasting organization.

A half to two thirds of the staff of the major foreign bureaus of TASS are still KGB officers; in some cases they are heads of the bureaus, TASS veteran Alexandr Zhebin wrote in "Agents of the Telegraph Agency," published by *Moscow news*. If there are two correspondents in a country, one of them is certainly not a journalist. And the secret service is still a large factor in forming the staff of the foreign bureaus. The author personally knows that a KGB officer has been a head of the department of cadres for appointments abroad for the last twenty years at least. It is no wonder that the interests of the special service are given the first priority. A good journalist is not considered the best candidate to work as a partner with a KGB officer: the difference between their materials is too visible to the local authorities. Besides, a real professional is not easily managed. As one of the most recent examples of this TASS bias toward KGB people, a new bureau in Seoul opened late in 1991. All the agency gets from there is accounts of articles in two English language newspapers published for foreigners.[13] The interests of information supply are sacrificed for the secret service for one reason: the total government control of all spheres of life.

The dependence of the media people in this country on the state is complete. Those on the very top are no more free than rank and file journalists. After the August putsch that was supported by the State TV and Radio Company, its chairman, Leonid Kravchenko, was dismissed. In an interview soon after that, he said that he "became a pawn in this grandioso chess game." He also revealed that until the very putsch the leading mass media continued to get directives from the Central Committee of the Communist Party as they used to. Every week their heads were invited to various meetings including those of the Secretariat. "Instructions, operative commissions were a norm. We have got used to it and took it for granted," said Kravchenko.[14]

After his resignation, Michail Nenashev, whose last state position was as minister of information and press of the USSR (formerly Goskompechat) wrote about "an epoch, that has formed several generations of the complaint," about the "psychology of slaves" and "thoughtless obedience." He titled his article "Professionalism as a victim of thoughtless obedience."[15] This idea is very different from the one he defended a while ago: that limiting the staff of the media to professionals would be undemocratic.

The mass media in this country suffer double consequences of the long history of totalitarian control. The first is evident: journalists' inclination to align themselves with power institutions. They still work not for the audience but for the powers that be, on whom their careers depend. They are associated with the authorities, speak on behalf of the authorities, and consider themselves important and influential because of those ties. For most of the media, the public still does not matter as it did not matter under Communist rule.

Another consequence is less evident but more ugly. Now that the mass media are being commercialized, the absence of professional standards and ethical principles has brought about widespread corruption. With the extensive introduction of advertising that corruption has exploded. As mentioned, the high level of corruption at the All-Union State Television and Radio Company (now Ostankino) has been openly admitted by its chairman, Yegor Yakovlev.

Yakovlev spoke of commercials but the problem is not limited to this sphere. Some interviews and entire business programs that audiences perceive as factual reporting (they are not identified otherwise) are funded by money that goes to the company or directly into the pockets of the TV team.

Something of this kind would ruin the reputation and career of a Western journalist forever and would be harmful to the medium in general. In this country, it is a widespread practice and not only on television. But who cares? Corruption is a phenomenon that has infiltrated all levels of power and all institutions. As academician Georgi Arbatov, an adviser of six consecutive governments in this country, pointed out, "In the new power structures corruption is almost legalized and boundless."[16] Roughly speaking, there are two modes of behavior among the media people in this country: some follow the traditional way of supporting the political powers and enjoy the benefits it can provide; others profit directly from the new enterpreneurs. This is a sick society and the mass media cannot be healthier than the system as a whole.

These are some of the first, bitter lessons the society can learn from the experiences of the mass media during the last several years. Getting rid of totalitarian control does not yet mean becoming free. It will be a long time before it becomes a common understanding in the media that to be free is in some sense more difficult than to be dependent because it presupposes individual choice and individual responsibility. A strong basis for press freedom is real professionalism, which implies high ethical standards, objectivity, social responsibility, and simple, elementary honesty.

Now that the whole world is so sympathetic to the changes that are going on in this country, the media professionals from Western democracies might help their colleagues here recognize these problems and solve them. A new type of journalism education to replace the old model of the press as an element of the totalitarian ideological system; training of young Russian journalists "in the field"—in American editorial offices and television studios; current translation and publication in Russian of basic American textbooks on mass communications—these are the first steps.

We are building a new media system from the very foundation, and that will take considerable effort and a long time. It is a serious job not only for the media themselves but for the society as a whole. As John McMillan, former publisher of the *Observer-Dispatch* in Utica, New York, once told me, the United States took two hundred years to develop the media system they have.

Nobody can say for sure how long the process will take in this country. But what creates some optimism is the fact that now we can learn from working models of free media around the globe—something the United States could not do two centuries ago.

What we basically need is to rediscover the human rights and freedoms that the whole world takes for granted. We were deprived of them for several generations. In this country, freedom must first become a state of mind. Only then can it become a state of society.

NOTES

1. *Nezavisimaya gazeta*, January 31, 1992.

2. *Radio Free Europe/Radio Liberty Daily Report*, January 7, 1991.

3. *Commersant*, No. 44, 1991, p.11.

4. *Radio Free Europe/Radio Liberty Daily Report*, March 28, 1991.

5. *Radio Free Europe/Radio Liberty Daily Report*, February 12, 1991; December 4, 1990.

6. Vera Tolz, Central Media Wage Propaganda Campaign against Lithuania. Report on the USSR. Radio Liberty. April 13, 1990, p. 3.

7. *The New York Times*, January 18, 1991; *Radio Free Europe/Radio Liberty Daily Report*, January 17, 1991.

8. *Izvestiya*, February 2, 1991; *Radio Free Europe/Radio Liberty Daily Report*, February 8, 1991.

9. *Izvestiya*, November 11, 1991.

10. *Izvestiya*, February 11, 1992.

11. *Stolitsa*, No. 2, 1991, p. 28.

12. *Moscow news*, No. 37, 1991, p. 4.

13. Alexandr Zhebin, Agenti telegrafnogo agentstva. *Moscow news*, No. 6, 1992, p. 20.

14. Leonid Kravchenko, Ya staralsya ne zadavat lishnich voprosov. *Komsomolskaya pravda*, September 20, 1991.

15. Michail Nenashev, Professionalism kak zhertva bezdumnogo poslushania. *Nwzavisimaya gazeta*, January 9, 1992.

16. *Nezavisimaya gazeta*, February 11, 1992.

2

THE PRESS IS FREE...

DOWN WITH NON-PARTY WRITERS

Freedom of the press was originally proclaimed by the Constitution of the Soviet Union but like the other freedoms this one existed only as a propaganda motto that had nothing to do with the reality.

Several years ago, nothing was easier than describing the structure of the print press in the Soviet Union. It was an absolutely centralized system. Its ideological purity was strictly controlled on all levels by the Communist party, and its physical existence was supported by government budgets and supplies.

Most numerous and visible were newspapers published by the party committees and the Soviets of People's Deputies, starting at the national level, where they had separate publications, and going down to the lower ones, where all local authorities had a joint publication. This vertical structure, officially and directly controlled by the party, was supplemented by a wholly obedient pyramid of Comsomol publications, plus newspapers and journals issued by public organizations such as the Union of Writers or the Committee of Soviet Women. Of these the most influential was the All-Union Council of Trade Unions.

Formally independent, in reality these associations were totally dominated by the party cadre and party ideology. Trade and in-house newspapers could be added to the list of publications but that would only mean an increase in numbers not in diversity of opinions.

The Communist party exercised diversified means of control over the mass media system, both tactical and strategic. In this hierarchical system, party committees and their newspapers had not only the right but the obligation to supervise all other publications at the same or lower level.

Every editor-in-chief had to present periodic plans for newspaper publications and campaigns to the appropriate party committee for approval. Later, he or she was obliged to report how the plans were fulfilled. The regularity of those contacts depended on the level of the publication: the higher the level, the tougher the control. For example, the plan for an issue of *Komsomolskaya pravda* and the topics of all articles were approved daily by the Central Committee of Comsomol, a youth organization of the Communist party. It is no wonder that the Soviet media were always late with their information: everything had to be approved, not just by the editor but by higher authorities.

The press was entirely subordinate to the party both on an everyday and on a long-term basis. All editors-in-chief were selected and appointed by the party committees and fully dependent on them.

A party committee had, depending on its level, a department, a sector, or at least an instructor supervising the mass media in the area of its responsibility. If it was, for example, a regional committee, it controlled not just its own newspaper and other publications at the same level but also district newspapers, and the way the local Communist authorities supervised them.

Regional party committee apparatchiks and staffers of its official publication reviewed district newspapers. Some of those reviews were published but mostly they were used to direct, instruct, and reprimand editors at regular meetings. Recommendations given there were not of an advisory but of an obligatory character. Editors who dared to disobey risked losing their job, but that rarely happened. These were the standard approaches and procedures used at all layers of the Communist party structure, both below and above the regional level, to exercise operational, tactical control.

Strategic control was implemented primarily by what was called "pursuing cadre policy" and party discipline. Cadre policy, to put it simply, is the promotion of ideologically and politically (and, as a rule, personally) reliable people to head all kinds of organizations and enterprises: from director of a state farm or editor of a town newspaper to minister of agriculture or chairman of the State Committee for Publishing. Those people were all called *nomenklatura* but there were different levels, from that of the Central Committee of the Party to the local level.

Cadre politics was the very cornerstone of the system; it kept everything everywhere under control, from the top to the very bottom. It also secured for the Communist leaders on all levels the loyalty of their appointees since they depended on the party apparatus for their promotion. And within any institution, no cadre decision could be taken without the approval of a secretary of a primary party organization.

As cadre policy ensured obedience of officials on all levels, rank and file Communists were strictly controlled by party discipline. According to the Party Charter, once a decision was formally made, nobody had a right to question it, only an obligation to fulfill. The rule, of course, was not limited to resolutions approved within a party organization. Resolutions of an upper level party committee were mandatory for all the Communists in its territory. This means that any decision could be imposed from the top without risk of challenge.

This system of total control penetrated all spheres of life in the Soviet Union. But in the mass media, which was considered part of the Communist party ideological machinery, it was tougher than anywhere else. This does not mean, as is often interpreted in Western countries, that every journalist was obliged to be a party member. But most joined and those who did not were handicapped. Young people could be admitted to the media without being members but it was taken for granted that to stay there one needed, as a rule, to join the party.

The common opinion in the West that membership was necessary for promotion is true, but not there is more. There were too many Communists for everyone to occupy an important position, whether journalists, engineers, or teachers. But for all the rank and file, membership in the party was a kind of a mark that you were accepted and trusted by the system. One could do without this token in other fields that were far enough from politics and ideology but in the media he or she would feel uncomfortable as an outsider.

Joining the party has never been easy for the intelligentsia although it tended to be more active than the other strata of the population. The so-called proletarian character of the party was artificially cultivated not just by widely opening it to workers and farmers but by recruiting and persuading them to join. Meanwhile, the access was limited for the intelligentsia and people competed to be admitted, some on a waiting list for years.

This was one of the most deeply rooted and fundamental manifestations of an anti-intellectual trend that was thoroughly inculcated by the Communist ideologists and started even before the October Revolution. In the party rhetoric that was dominant in the political and social life of the entire country and actually determined its mentality the proletariat was labeled a *hegemon,* or an overlord, and the intelligentsia was considered to be inferior to it. The official definition was "a non-class strata," but in everyday life people often scornfully referred to it as to "a rotten intelligentsia."

Praising the working class with its presumed superiority made it easier to manipulate the masses. But on the other hand, the authorities had always been suspicious of the intelligentsia as a potential source of dissent. Intellectual freedom has never existed in this country, neither as a reality nor as a theoretical notion. But if in the totalitarian society there was something the authorities could not keep under full control, however much

they would have liked to, it was people's minds. The powers that be tried
to subordinate the intelligentsia by different means: by humiliating it, by
trying to cultivate in it low self-esteem, by bribing it, and by repressing
it. And, in general, they were quite successful.

Now the whole country is paying for the success of the authorities in
bringing the people down to the lowest common denominator. It is paying
for the shameful state of its humanities and the backwardness in many
fields of its science. The country is now held back by the low cultural and
technological level, by the low level of life, and, worst of all, by the
inability of political and economic leaders to break the old patterns and
solve old problems.

Several generations of Soviet people were raised under the pressure
of Communist dogmas. According to them, party decrees and resolutions
had always determined social and political development. That is why
professionals, people of independent thinking, have never been in real
demand in the system. Ideology was the main criterion that determined
their acceptability to the power structures. It is no wonder that journalists, whose role was to be a mouthpiece of the party, first of all had
to be obedient.

It is no wonder that the political dissent in the Soviet Union in the
pre-perestroika period was strongest among scientists, physicists, and
mathematicians, who were less indoctrinated by Marxist ideology and
more independent of party control in their daily lives. There were also
expressions of dissent among people in the arts. Though artistic productions were under ideological supervision and the public could not gain
access to them without official permission, still people in the arts did not
have to deal with the system on an everyday basis.

But journalists were at the opposite end of the social scale, where party
control was overwhelming. Education, selection, and promotion were
directed to one goal: to keep the entire media structure uniform, manageable, and obedient. Its instrumental, supplementary role in Communist party ideological and political activities was openly proclaimed as
the basic underlying principle of the press in the Soviet Union. It is a
"party-minded" principle, that the foremost obligation of the media is to
defend the interests of the Communist party and support its politics.

It was proclaimed by Lenin and maintained in a number of his works
that were required reading in all the schools of journalism in the USSR.
The most important of Lenin's works is considered to be his article "Party
organization and party literature," which determined the future, not only
of the underground Bolshevik press, but of all the mass media of the
Soviet Union for over seventy years.

In 1905, at the time of the First Russian Revolution, Lenin wrote:

> In contradistinction to bourgeois customs, to the profit-making, commer-
> cialized bourgeois press, to bourgeois literary careerism and individualism,

"aristocratic anarchism" and drive for profit, the socialist proletariat must put forward the principle of *Party literature,* must develop this principle, and put it into practice as fully and completely as possible.

What is this principle of Party literature?... Literature can not be a means of enriching individuals or groups: it cannot, in fact, be an individual undertaking, independent of the common cause of the proletariat. Down with non-partisan writers!... Literature must become *part* of the common cause of the proletariat.... Literature must become a component of organized, planned and integrated Social-Democratic Party work.[1]

Journalism students could recite this quotation almost by heart, so often was it repeated in different courses. What they were not told was that by "party literature" Lenin originally meant only party publications: "We are discussing Party literature and its subordination to Party control."[2]

But when the Bolsheviks came to power, they soon prohibited all the other political organizations and suspended their publications. Bolsheviks aimed at establishing their own brainwashing system, which they entirely controlled, and they were quite successful in it.

Ideological managers extended this principle not just to the press and literature, but to the other fields of the liberal arts, too. This concept enabled the Soviet leaders and the party structure as a whole to supervise all sources of intellectual, moral, emotional, and psychological influence on the public, or at least those intended for mass distribution. Cadres selected by the Communist party apparat were in charge of this system. Books and periodicals could not be published, theater ventures could not be produced, paintings and sculptures could not be exhibited, movies could not be projected without the approval of those state gatekeepers. Cultural departments at different levels, from the Ministry of Culture to the towns and districts, exercised those functions in respect to the liberal arts.

The famous Glavlit censored all kinds of literature. It was not difficult to control everything that was published because all the printing plants belonged either to the party or to the state. There was a censor in each plant (or a number of censors, depending on the size of an enterprise). Literally nothing, including invitations to a student's party or other equally innocent forms, could be printed without their stamp and signature.

The system of censorship that embraced both the media and the arts was just one more mechanism for preserving the totally controlled system. In ideology and propaganda, as in nuclear power stations, there were many defense systems. A station could probably operate safely with fewer of them but the risk was too high and so to be on safe ground, it was preferable to have them all.

The same multilevel control was practiced in the media. If one considers the strict ideological and political supervision by the party nomenklatura that enveloped the field, having censorship was a kind of an extra, a luxury, however paradoxical this might sound. But it was necessary for the authorities to feel assured that the system would not fail under any conditions. For a totalitarian system, this nuclear power station mode of organization (control of control of control) was natural; it was its mode of existence.

THE LAW ON THE PRESS: A STEP TO FREEDOM

The Law on the Press and the Other Mass Media that was adopted by the Soviet legislature in June 1990 and went into force in August was the first legal document regulating the media in the history of the Soviet Union.

Of course, proclamation by the law that "the Press and the other mass media are free" did not guarantee freedom of the press. But its very existence primarily indicated that the monopoly of Communist ideology was over. It was actually an acknowledgment that mass media management was no longer to be "the party cause" and that they would be regulated not by party decrees and resolutions but by legal mechanisms.

The history of the law is long and complicated. Several drafts were prepared. A discussion of this sensitive issue provoked a clash between the democratic forces in the Supreme Soviet of the USSR and the old party nomenklatura both in the legislature and in the Central Committee of the Communist party. The party apparat did its best to fashion a law that would conserve its privileges but the parliamentarian working group on the law rejected the draft approved by the Ideological Commission and the Politburo. The group accepted as a basis for its work a more liberal version drawn up by a group of young lawyers of the Institute of State and Law of the USSR Academy of Sciences.

The highest party officials, including a member of the Politburo responsible for ideological issues, Vadim Medvedev, personally tried to influence the working group to change the document. Medvedev attempted to exclude some of the most democratic clauses, such as elimination of preliminary censorship and the authorization for a private citizen to be a founder of a news medium. Originally, the publication of the draft in the press was prohibited.

The group did not yield to pressure. The head of the group, Nikolai Fyodorov, complained that one of its members, Georgi Shakhnazarov (an assistant to the secretary general of the Central Committee of the CPSU until the resignation of Michail Gorbachev from this post), when introducing the document to the legislature in November 1989 presented the disputed articles in the form advocated by Medvedev.[3]

The presidium of the Supreme Soviet made its contribution to prolonging and complicating the procedure of passage of the law by the Parliament, too. After the first hearing of the draft, the working group which was part of a committee on lawmaking, legality, and law and order, was dissolved. In its place a commission of the Presidium was set up to work on the draft.

Those in the commission were not members of the Supreme Soviet but government officials, directly interested in the results of the discussion. Among them were the chairmen of the State Committee for Television and Radio Broadcasting and the State Committee on Publishing Houses, Printing Plants and the Book Trade. In the Soviet Union, where the separation of powers was not known and everything was controlled by a symbiosis of the Communist party and the state, drafting of laws to serve its own interests by the government bureaucracy was an everyday practice.

In this case, it did not work and the legislators managed to push through the initial draft. But the nomenklatura were at least successful in delaying the adoption of the long-awaited law for six months.

The two points that the party officials struggled against most persistently are fundamental to the new law and the mass media. Censorship is not allowed. The right to establish a mass medium is granted to the Soviets and other state bodies; political parties, public organizations, mass movements, and artistic unions; cooperative, religious, and other associations; working collectives; and the citizens of the USSR.[4]

The law introduced a "registration principle" that applies to both the new and the old media. The authorities are obliged to register a medium within a month of its application. A few reasons for refusal to register are listed in the law.

New publications started appearing in the Soviet Union in the period of perestroika long before the press law was adopted. Legally they were prohibited, but they kept publishing anyway and the authorities did not really try to suspend them. They appeared first in the Baltics and then spread throughout the country. Sometimes their distributors complained that the police did not allow them to sell the papers. But the government did not take any serious measures to stop publication, though it definitely could have. Passage of the law provided a legal basis for the existence of an independent press and stimulated its flourishing.

By March 1991, 1773 All-Union publications were registered, half of them new: 803 were founded by state institutions, 233 by editorial collectives and publishing houses, 291 by public associations, 27 by parties, 19 by religious organizations, some by cooperatives and businesses, 241 by private persons.[5] Probably the most successful and the largest of the independent newspapers is *Nezavisimaya gazeta*, founded by the Moscow City Council and edited by a journalist, Vitaly Tretyakov, who used to work for the *Moscow news*.

For the Soviet media the law was a highly significant step from glasnost to freedom of the press. But it was just the first step and it inevitably reflected all the complexities of the situation in the country and the internal problems of the media themselves. However important any law is by itself, its impact is weakened if it ignores political and economic realities.

The law guarantees to everyone the right to launch a news medium but it overlooks the fact that all the publishing facilities in the country, as well as the electronic media and networks for their distribution, are monopolies of the Communist party or of the state. "Critics of the law seem to be right in saying that until such time as the existing publishing houses and electronic media are freed from the CPSU and government control, private publishing houses are permitted, and paper is sold on the free market, only marginal changes in the situation of the media are likely."[6]

The compromising nature of the law could not help provoking disagreements and conflicts in the process of its implementation. All the media were supposed to be registered by their "founders." There were no problems with new publications, but the registration of existing publications provoked quite a number of conflicts. Basically, those conflicts emerged because of the ambiguity in precisely locating an owner in this country where almost everything belonged to the party-state symbiosis. When the law granted "working collectives" the right to establish news media, staffers of many long existing newspapers and magazines, especially the most popular and profitable, applied for registration as their "founders."

The law did not give an exact legal definition of "a founder" but gave it important rights: a founder determines the political line of a publication and has the right to appoint and dismiss the editor-in-chief and to suspend publication. That is why battles for the right to become founders have been so crucial.

On one hand, the press law has been an important step from totalitarian control of the media to legal regulation of it. On the other hand, it lays the foundation for redistribution of control over the media on vaguely defined grounds in pure Bolshevik style.

It is highly doubtful that a "collective" can be a good manager. There are always at least two dangers in this form of control: one, that because of disagreements inside a collective, an enterprise will become unworkable; another, that an administration will usurp all the power and manipulate the collective for its own benefit. Both dangers are quite possible. A working collective that is a founder can easily be exploited so that it doesn't really democratize a news medium but redistributes power, dismisses former controllers to serve the interests of a new group, and even covers some of its machinations with ownership in the absence of a legally defined proprietor.

The newly founded publications don't have this problem. But for those that have been in existence for a long while it is a problem of redistribution of control and ownership. Managers of state owned enterprises, especially if they have support of the government, can easily become actual owners of real estate, news media or factories at a symbolic price. While in the Western countries control of money serves as a basis of political power, now in Russia, political connections and access to state ownership are easily converted into private ownership. The process of the restructuring of ownership is far from being completed, and it is no wonder that it provokes quite a number of conflicts: there are many important interests involved. Tomorrow's money elite is being formed from the yesterday's Communist elite on the basis of its access to state property. They privatize it according to the rules they wrote for themselves.

Quite a number of conflicts emerged because the law did not state directly whether its term *founder* is applicable to the existing media. It is hard to believe that this was an evil plan by the initiators of the law. It seems most probable that the lawmakers meant to regulate the working system and provide for its development but not to destroy it. Nevertheless, the effect is that they planted the seeds of future conflict.

This turned out to be a crucial point because not only the new media but all media had to be registered by a founder. All organizations, state, political, and public that had been publishing newspapers and magazines for years and years, naturally considered themselves their founders. They thought it was just a different denomination for their position. Although this idea seemed quite logical to them, its opponents disagreed.

They maintained that the idea of a founder is quite a new notion, that no organization has the right to pretend that it already has this stature, and that no historical claims should be considered. Everything starts here and now from the very beginning, from a zero point. It was, of course, a good pretext to get rid of the bothersome control quickly and radically in a neo-Bolshevik revolutionary manner, but these arguments were not convincing.

In a number of cases an actual publisher and a working collective managed to reach an agreement to become joint founders. In rare cases an actual publisher allowed a publication to do what it liked. This happened to the *Moscow news*, which managed to convince Novosti press agency to release it. The agency was involved in foreign propaganda and for years the newspaper that it had been publishing in several languages for foreigners was not successful. But at the time of perestroika when Yegor Yakovlev was appointed its editor-in-chief, the Russian language edition of the *Moscow news* became highly popular as one of the most outspoken voices of democracy. However, the management of Novosti Press Agency was not interested in the Russian edition that was most popular.

After independence, the newspaper staff resisted the temptation to become its own founder. Some well known political and cultural personalities were invited to become founders of the *Moscow news*. But this is an exception. And although for the moment it appears to be a more civilized way of dealing with media issues, it doesn't address the basic problem of media ownership: a founder is not a shareholder.

The staff of the Leningrad *Smena*, one of the oldest newspapers in the country which has always been published by the regional Comsomol committee, applied for registration of the newspaper as its founder. The journalists conducted a one-day hunger strike to pressure the authorities. It is a local publication and a decision had to be made at the local level.

But the Ministry of Press and Mass Information of Russia interfered and registered *Smena* as a newspaper founded by a working collective. The Russian government members who were in opposition to Gorbachev's central authority assisted the troublemaker that could help to widen their own support. It did the same in a number of other cases where publications for some reason had difficulty in registration with the All-Union authorities.

Because of the new law, collectives of several well known and successful literary periodicals that had been published by the writers' organizations of the USSR and republics decided to become founders of their publications. *Oktyabr* magazine which was published by the Russian Writers' Union, had no problem with registration by its staff at the republican Ministry of Press. They hoped to prevent conflict by quick action: the new status of the magazine was formalized on the very first day of registration. If it hadn't been, the highly conservative leaders of the Russian Writers' Union, who had already unsuccessfully tried to get rid of the editor of *Oktyabr*, Anatoly Ananyev, would hardly have let the magazine get away so easily. To characterize the attitude of the Union's leadership to glasnost, it is enough to mention that the chairman of the Union, Yuri Bondarev, said that it had done more harm to the Soviet Union than the German invasion in World War II had.

A weekly newspaper, *Literaturnaya gazeta*, and the monthlies, *Znamya* and *Yunost*, which also intended to become their own founders, entered into a conflict with the board of the USSR Writers' Union, which had been their publisher. The *Znamya* situation was even more complicated, because there were two more claimants to it: *Pravda* publishing house, which provided the magazine with an office, equipment, and printing facilities and kept its staff on the payroll; and the staff of the *Pravda* printing plant. But the two withdrew their claims later.

For decades, the Union exercised strict ideological control over those publications on behalf of the Communist party and used their profits. It is no wonder that when the press law was enacted, the periodicals used the opportunity the law offered to get rid of this control. Although these were the All-Union publications, which had to be registered with the USSR State Committee for Publishing Houses, Printing Plants, and the Book Trade (Goskompechat), all of them were registered with the RSFSR Ministry of the Press as founded by their staffs. The ministry did the same to some other national (All-Union) magazines: *Inostrannaya literatura*, *Druzhba narodov*, and *Novy mir* (jointly with the USSR Literary Fund).

The role of the Ministry of the Press and Mass Information of Russian in restructuring control over the media in the Soviet Union after the adoption of the press law was much more important than could be expected and than was actually provided for by the press law. In the period when the Soviet Union was still in existence and its officials were in power, this institution of the Russian government had usurped some of the central authorities' responsibilities. By those means it undermined Union authority and also ensured government support of those media that it favored in conflicts.

The staff of an outspoken liberal weekly, *Ogonyok*, became engaged in a conflict with the *Pravda* publishing house. Both intended to become founders. Evidently, *Pravda* had all the rights because the magazine was established in the middle 1920s as its publication. It could have been that *Ogonyok* wanted to gain editorial independence. An outsider's impression was that by the late 1980s the magazine at that time, one of the most popular publications in the country, which with *Moscow news* became a symbol of the era of glasnost, had already gained independence. Probably, for a magazine that was quite successful from a business point of view gaining financial independence was an equally strong stimulus.

The publishers yielded to the demands of the staff and it appeared that the working collective had won. But it was evident that as soon as the magazine needed to be printed somewhere and had no real alternative to the *Pravda* printing plant, the publishers would take their revenge. And they did.

Ogonyok was no longer a part of the publishing house. It had to make a contract with *Pravda*, and the printing plant managers could dictate terms. Although the working collective believed that its role was decisive, the administration of the magazine signed a secret agreement that ensured *Pravda* about 70 percent of the profit from the magazine and 100 percent of the profit from its book supplement.

Several months after the magazine was registered, on the eve of 1991, the chairman of the council of the working collective, Vladimir Vigilyansky, in an open letter to his colleagues wrote, "The working collective as a founder turned out to be only a cover, a screen for the authoritarian administration." As a result of numerous financial infringements that were thoroughly concealed by the magazine officials, the working collective, he said, was "robbed."[7]

There was a sharp contradiction between the principles the magazine proclaimed in its pages and the practices of its administration.

Struggle for human rights turned out to be violation of rights of the members of the working collective. Struggle for glasnost in the society does not correspond to back-stage intrigues in the editorial office. Unmasking of corruption and the shadow economy in the country goes parallel to secret dealings. The demand to depoliticize public and state institutions is in contradiction to the fact that three quarters of the editorial board and the entire top administration are members of the Communist party.[8]

The administration did not react to the protests of the staffers. They forced a large group of fourteen leading editors and journalists, who had made *Ogonyok* a platform for glasnost, resign. After they left, the editorial board became 100 percent Communist. Knowing that revelations of this kind could be ruinous to the magazine's reputation, they kept silent for a long time. Not until the next autumn, about year after this mass resignation, Vladimir Vigilyansky published his letter in a Moscow magazine, *Stolitsa* (Capital), and gave it an interview.[9]

This scandal, although it may not be typical, demonstrates how easy it is for a small group of administrators to seize control of a publication and manipulate the working collective. It is evident that the top management sought to get rid of external control in order to establish its own internal control. This has nothing to do with the drive for independence and freedom of the press.

From the point of view of economics, it is a deadlock, too. "Collective newspapers" cannot be more efficient than the collective farms, which generally were failures. The authors of the press law evidently thought that introducing collectives as possible founders to break the Communist party dictatorship would be a progressive measure. The idea could work only if the staffers would buy shares and become individual owners. But the way it is done now is not a step to independence of the newspapers; it's a concession to neo-Bolshevik ideology.

What could really help freedom of the press is the inclusion in the law of anti-monopoly measures to break the party-government monopoly on the means of production and distribution of the mass media. This has not been done.

The law states, "Monopolization of any mass medium (press, radio, television and others) is not allowed." But the government never directs this clause against itself. Besides, it falls again to the executive authorities to determine what exactly is meant by monopolization and what kind of measures can be taken against it. And cross ownership (of multiple media) is not mentioned at all.

One more point related to the status of founder produced disagreements in the process of registration and was interpreted in different ways. At the beginning, Goskompechat refused to register publications of political parties because the Law on the Parties had not yet been adopted. It implied that the parties first had to register themselves and only after that their newspapers. Of course, it did not make much difference to *Pravda*, which was published in any case. But it did make a difference to new political parties that planned their publications.

Parties found ways to register rather easily in this case. Some registered party newspapers with private persons as founders. The Russian Ministry of Press offered another option: it declared that it would register these publications because the press law mentions political parties among possible founders. Thus, the Ministry of the Press had outplayed Goskompechat again, adding to disruption of the Center.

The Law on the Press had eliminated preliminary censorship. But here, again, matters were not that simple. The tone of newspaper headlines varied from the euphoric FAREWELL TO CENSORSHIP to the more realistic CENSORSHIP LIFTED, CENSORS REMAIN or WHAT IS OUR CENSOR LEAVING FOR?[10] The greatest achievement was that ideological censorship was lifted. Actually it had been gradually declining since the emergence of glasnost, long before the press law was adopted. But state and military secrets remained, and it became the editor's responsibility to see that they were not made public. Disclosure of secret data was prohibited by the press law.

Elements of political censorship related to publication of sensitive information that the authorities would like to conceal continued in the official media, too, although the diversity of media voices made censorship more difficult.

The conflict in *Izvestiya* in January 1991 caused by the authorities' attempt to get rid of the first deputy editor-in-chief, Igor Golembiovsky, publicized some cases of censorship exercised under glasnost after the Law on the Press was in Force. The immediate reason for the attempt to send Golembiovsky as far away as Spain to serve as a correspondent for several years was his signing of a strongly worded protest against the Soviet crackdown in Lithuania published by *Moscow news*.

Chairman of the Supreme Soviet of the USSR (*Izvestiya* was its publication), Anatoly Lukyanov, suggested making Golembiovsky a correspondent in Spain. Apparently Lukyanov misinformed the members of the Presidium of the Supreme Soviet when he asked them to approve the editor's replacement by saying that Golembiovsky agreed to go to Spain voluntarily. The journalists of *Izvestiya* urgently demanded a meeting with Lukyanov and Gorbachev; they said that the public would view Golembiovsky's replacement as the persecution of the independent media by the president.

At the staff meeting of *Izvestiya*, nearly two hundred people unanimously voted to demand that Golembiovsky remain in office. They also accused Editor-in-Chief Yefimov of constantly removing from the newspaper articles that did not coincide with the views of the Communist party. Yefimov had pulled out several stories about the attack of the Soviet troops on the Vilnius TV tower after they had already been laid out in the newspaper. The presses were already running when Yefimov had apparently pulled out a story that he considered too critical of a 100,000 people anti-Gorbachev rally outside the Kremlin. Thousand of copies of the newspaper printed within the first half-hour were destroyed.[11]

Censorship was eliminated but the government institution that carried it out survived, though under a new sign. The famous Glavlit (Chief Administration for Protection of State Secrets in Print) was transformed into GUOT (Chief Administration for Protection of State Secrets in the Press and Other News Media). Even the name is almost the same; only the abbreviation is different—Glavlit was too odious; it was necessary to get rid of it. Typically the head of Glavlit was smoothly shifted to the corresponding position in GUOT.

In the Soviet Union, secrets were not limited to state and military issues as everywhere else and not to ideological dogmas. In the democratic countries most information is available to the society and only a small part is classified; in the Soviet Union the proportion was just the opposite. Every ministry and every government body had secrets of its own, and all of them were closed to the news media and public opinion. Those secrets had nothing to do with national interests. In most cases, information was classified to conceal inefficiency and misdeeds. All those secrets were designed to guarantee that in the mass media, the Soviet Union would appear to be a prosperous society with popular leadership, an efficient economy, a high level of life, a low level of crime, flourishing culture, interethnic harmony, and so on.

It could be expected that the prohibition of censorship would at least reveal ministerial secrets but this did not happen. Less than a month after the press law was enacted, editors throughout the country received a new document from the former Glavlit. It was just two pages long and classified "Secret." Its circulation twenty thousand and each copy was numbered. The paper was titled "On changing 'the list of information that may not be published,' 1990 edition."[12]

The secret document listed many items that could not be made public by the Soviet media (and remember, these were only revisions to be added to the existing book). Among them were facts and figures regarding animals stricken with foot-and-mouth disease caused by an exotic strain of the virus, cattle stricken with rinderpest and contagious pleuropneumonia, horses stricken with the African plague and Venezuelan encephalomyelitis, and sheep stricken with Rift Valley fever and Nairobi disease.

It was probably the veterinary authorities who did not want this information published.

Railroad management had its own interest in the list of secrets. It intended to hide data on wear and tear of railroad cars—probably so that the public would not become alarmed about the safety of railroad travel.

The military officials took care not to reveal undesirable information, too. It prohibited the publishing of summary data (covering military units, military-educational institutions, or higher-level entities) concerning the unsatisfactory state of military discipline among personnel of the USSR Armed Forces, the number of crimes and convictions, and extraordinary incidents (murder; suicide; injury, death, or disablement of people; maiming; desertion; theft of weapons and military hardware; violation of the regulations governing alert status, and any manifestation of group discontent by servicemen). Concealing this information obviously had nothing to do with the strategic interests of the country. Only the military bureaucracy was interested in masking the level of crime and disorder in the army. Nevertheless, all these data were on the list of censored information after censorship had been formally abolished.

Officially, the Council of Ministers determined exactly what was secret. But there was always an open door for departmental interests. Ministries were welcome to classify any unfavorable information. Here is just one example to illustrate how potentially dangerous to the society this manipulation of information can be. After the Chernobyl disaster the Council of Ministers at the request of the nuclear energy officials classified all the data about the incident and its consequences. It was not until the late 1980s that some Chernobyl statistics were leaked to the press. Before that, both people who were directly affected by the catastrophe and the society as a whole were uninformed.

Not only the Council of Ministers but GUOT is entitled "to draft out and publish on the basis of the constitutional norms and the acting legislation a list of data banned for publication."[13] According to its head, Vladimir Boldirev, among other functions, GUOT also controls materials going abroad and coming in from other countries.[14]

After this long digression about what is considered secret, how a list of secrets is compiled, and what the responsibilities of a censorship department are, it is not easy to remember that this discussion started with the topic of the elimination of censorship by the press law. The problem for the editors was that, although there were no censors around any longer, secrets existed and responsibility for preserving them was now theirs. The editors had neither dealt with those problems themselves nor employed experts on those issues. GUOT has offered the mews media "consulting" to determine whether there is information in their materials that is banned from publication.

"Consulting" is absolutely voluntary, but that does not mean that editors have a real choice whether to use these services or not. "The list of information that may not be published" is itself a secret book, too, and only censors have access to it. As a result, a number of editors (and not only those of conservative publications) preferred to sign agreements with censors to protect themselves from the prospect of criminal charges. In accordance with the press law, no censorship was imposed from the top. Censors were invited to be consultants—entirely voluntarily, of course. The old censorship was free; the new consulting was paid for by the newspapers and, consequently, by the readers.

The editor of *Nezavisimaya gazeta*, Vitaly Tretyakov, who did not follow suit, has ironically commented on the conduct of the leftist newspapers that enthusiastically fought for the elimination of censorship in the USSR but "today 'just in this case' left censors in their editorial offices."[15]

Of course, some confusion among media officials can be understood: the authorities keep playing their game of secrecy and its rules are not really known to anyone else. On the other hand, this confusion demonstrates that in demanding the abolition of censorship most editors did not realize that this freedom would inevitably entail new obligations and responsibilities, which would not be easy. The editors turned out to be unready for it and readily sacrificed their freedom for the sake of comfort and safety. Censorship is not allowed by the law but is actually practiced by mutual agreement.

Censorship has never disappeared, says Deputy Minister of the Press and Mass Information of RSFSR, Michail Fedotov who later became Minister. Several decrees and resolutions adopted by the Soviet government institutions after the press law was enacted were aimed at nullifiying the provisions abolishing censorship. The resolution on Glavlit called for the continuation of the organization and preserved many of its traditional functions. A resolution of Gosteleradio, the Ministry of Justice, and the Ministry of Communications concerning registration of new audio and video mass media gives government institutions the right to decide arbitrarily which news media should be registered and which not.[16]

In March 1991, the Committee on Glasnost of the USSR Supreme Soviet met to discuss implementation of the press law. The legislators also mentioned the necessity for quickly adopting a new law on the right to information. They stressed that a law was needed to clarify what information constitutes a state secret. The draft was supposed to be ready for public discussion by the beginning of 1991 but it was never published until the very collapse of the Union. Some participants in the discussion complain that the press law is often violated in the provinces, and the Soviet mass media have carried many reports about how local Communist officials have arbitrarily interfered in the work of the mass media.

The press law came about as a result of a compromise and it is no wonder that it has been criticized by both sides. Some commentators found that it did not give enough freedom; others said that it did not provide enough control. The latter point of view was typical of state officials who were raised in a fully loyal media environment and found it difficult to get used to the new realities.

Even a great reformer like Michail Gorbachev, as already mentioned, wanted to suspend the law because of the anti-government coverage of the events in Lithuania.

The top officials of the Soviet media establishment spoke in the USSR legislature during the discussion of this move. According to Leonid Kravchenko, who took over chairmanship of the Gosteleradio after Michail Nenashev left, plurality in the news media made it difficult for people to trust them; they were used to the old system.

The chairman of Goskompechat (former head of Gosteleradio), Michail Nenashev, said that the press law "needs to be corrected," in particular because it does not specify what organ must coordinate the work of the mass media. There is no mechanism for legal inspection, for analysis of how they observe their declared programs, he said. Many publications, complained the high official, are on their own and are not controlled by the state. Taking advantage of imperfections of the press law, they demonstrate subjectivity and partiality and conduct internecine struggles under the motto of independence. Nenashev seriously worried about loss of control over the mass media system by the power elite; that is why he planned the reorganization of Goskompechat.

His committee was concerned about the decrease in its power after the introduction of the press law, which aimed at liberating the Soviet media from the control of the Communist party and to some extent of the state. Nenashev stressed that his committee was dissatisfied with the one task assigned to it by the press law: that of registrating newspapers and periodicals. It is no wonder that the committee did not want to limit itself to this one function: it owned and controlled most of the publishing facilities in the Soviet Union in the name of the state.[17]

These complaints by the highest ranking government supervisors of the press, TV, and radio illustrate the tremendous progress of the media within the years of perestroika: they can no longer be manipulated. On the other hand, these comments prove that the desire of the authorities to tame and direct the news media has not been eradicated.

To some extent their statements reflect attitudes not only of the rulers but of a large part of the society. People were accustomed to reading biased, one-sided information, rather than facts they could interpret for themselves. Plurality in the mass media came as a shock to people who had lived in a one-dimensional world and did not have the habit of independent thinking.

However significant the adoption of the first press law was, probably its greatest significance was symbolic, as a recognition that the Communist party had no right to supervise the media system any longer. Although freedom of the press had been proclaimed, because of a number of practical obstacles, it appears to be more an ideal than a reality so far.

The law was created to fit the standards of lawmaking customary for the Soviet Union. Legislation here has not been based on the presumption of the priority of individual rights and freedoms. On the contrary, the state has allowed only as much freedom as it considered necessary. This gave rise to the basic rule of lawmaking in this country: what is not allowed is prohibited.

Probably the major omission from the law is that it does not provide for freedom of information for both the news media and individuals. People's right to know should be its most basic principle, guaranteed by freedom of the press. This is vitally important not only for the media but probably to a greater extent for the individuals and the society.

But to be realistic, in this country at that time, the legislature could hardly have produced a more progressive law. Its defects are evident, but nevertheless it has stimulated the development of the new media that will work to form a new society.

THE COMMUNIST PRESS IS TRYING TO SURVIVE

The problem of party ownership has been one of the most sensitive issues raised by the opposition in its struggle against the old nomenklatura. In a country with a low level of life, there was nothing easier than to arouse the outrage of the people by describing the privileges of the party apparatchiks. The legality of the party's profits and capital was fairly questioned. It was absolutely true that the party had free access to the state budget and resources and often abused them for its own sake and might.

By no means do I defend the misdoings of the party. It bears all the responsibility for bringing this country into a historical deadlock. Nevertheless, to demand nationalization or confiscation of the party property without any trial means to perpetuate the vicious circle of lawlessness, that has imprisoned the country since 1917. There will be neither democracy nor legality, only illusions of them, until this circle is broken.

The Communist party was an absolute ideological monopolist in the Soviet Union. It was the largest owner of printing plants. It was also the largest publisher. Although the party budget has never been known either by the citizens or by its rank and file members, the Party Charter listed profits of publishing as one of the major sources of its income, alongside membership dues and other activities.

Publishing houses that belonged to the Communist party (the largest were Pravda, Politizdat, and Plakat) enjoyed special treatment. Unlike any other enterprises, they did not pay taxes, nor did the party that received all the profits. Altogether, the administration of the Central Committee of the Communist Party supervised 57 percent of all the publishing facilities in the country. It had 114 publishing houses and 406 newspapers. Local Communist organizations published 3500 newspapers. Annually the party received about 1 billion rubles from publishing while membership dues brought it 1.2 billion.[18]

We have already described how the party apparat organized subscriptions to ensure high circulations and profits from newspapers and periodicals. As to the numerous books on Marxist ideology and Soviet politics that have been published in huge quantities, all the libraries throughout the country, as well as party committees on all levels, were obliged to buy them. Nevertheless, many copies were unsold and were recycled.

The financial losses from ideological production were made up by the profit from popular publications. Thus the Pravda publishing house tolerated the opposition magazine *Ogonyok* during perestroika because it generated an annual profit of about 70 million rubles.[19]

From the beginning of perestroika as the authority of the Communist party declined, its right to all the property that it managed was questioned more and more often. The first demands to breakup its ownership were issued from inside the party by representatives of different platforms, which claimed their share. At the 28th Congress of the Party, Michail Gorbachev managed to prevent its breakup.

Nevertheless, this did not mean that the subject was closed. The opposition late demanded the nationalization of party property.

For a long time, it has been a hot topic in political discussions and it still is. The most radical supporters of this point of view demand that the party return everything to the people. Others argue that fifty or seventy years of wrongs do not justify arbitrary rule and expropriation today. A court, they say, is the only institution that can solve the conflict.

In practical terms, the first institutions to challenge party control of the media system were the People's Soviets on different levels. They have always played a subsidiary role in the party-government structure, giving approval to all the bills initiated and drafted by the nomenklatura. But after the first free elections they started to develop into a separate branch of government.

The major problem of party ownership is identifying who really owns a particular newspaper or publishing house because within their history they may have changed hands. Michail Poltoranin, the minister of Press and Mass Information of Russia, quoted in the *Moscow news* a resolution of the Central Committee of the CPSU of February 1, 1967, which ordered subordination of all the regional, territorial, and republican newspaper and magazine publishing houses and their printing plants to the respective committees of the Communist party.[20]

In Kemerovo, the regional Soviet made an inventory of property of the party organization. The most crucial problem was ownership of the regional printing plant. In 1983, it was transferred to the regional Party Committee. The council estimated the profits that it could have received within those years at 4 million rubles and intended to charge the committee.

In Leningrad, the regional Communist Party Committee decided to keep the morning daily *Leningradskaya pravda* and to give the evening *Vecherni Leningrad* to the City Soviet. In 1990–1991, there were several attempts to strengthen and secure the control of the party organization over the major publishing house of the region, Lenizdat, either by turning it into a commercial structure under Communist control or by directly subordinating it to the Central Committee of the CPSU.

In the largest industrial city of the Urals, Sverdlovsk, the City Committee of the Communist party started a new periodical, *Spravedlivost* (Justice). The committee had been one of the founders of the largest regional newspaper, *Severni rabochii* but claimed that in the current political situation the paper did not give Sverdlovsk Communists enough space to air their views. In order to attract readers, the committee charged less for the paper than was charged for any other printed publication available in Sverdlovsk.

In the Ukrainian city Zaporozhje, the Party Committee, jointly with the leaders of the local government and industry, established the association Glasnost, which became a "founder" of the two largest newspapers, one regional and one for the city. This enabled nomenklatura to preserve control of the press after the Communist party was suspended.

In Kazakhstan the republican Committee of the Communist Party took over the two major dailies, one in the Russian language, the other one in Kazakh. They were formerly jointly owned by the republican Central Committee of the Party, the republican government, and the Supreme Soviet. The second secretary of the Central Committee, Vladislav Anufriev, told the editorial staff, "We need a newspaper like "Sovetskaya Rossiya." It is time to put a stop to pseudodemocracy, to any kind of Popovs and Sobchaks."[21] (Popov and Sobchak are democratic mayors of Moscow and Leningrad, respectively.)

The State Publishing Committee of Kazakhstan refused to register the independent newspaper *Social-Demokrat* on the grounds that it was an organ of the republican Social-Democratic party.

In Moscow, the City Soviet claimed that it was the legal owner of the two city newspapers, *Moskovskaya pravda* and *Vechernyaya Moskva*, because it had launched both of them, one in 1918, the other in 1923. They were taken over by the Party Committee in 1920 and 1931, respectively. The same was true of the printing plant. The council demanded the return of both the newspapers and the publishing facilities. In other words, the new political forces duplicated the methods of the old forces. However, the city party committee kept *Moskovskaya pravda* for itself.

Political opponents of Gorbachev and the Communist party as a whole considered arguments like those used by the Moscow legislature sufficient justification to nationalize party property. The lumpen society that came to power with the Bolsheviks considered it natural and fair to seize and share. The idea sounded quite attractive. But there were no trials to resolve the arguments legally.

Appealing to courts is not customary in this country and in this case the conflicts were solved without judicial interference. If there was anything good about those arguments, it was that the controversies were not ended by simply redistributing what already existed. Quite a number of new publications were launched by Soviets at different levels when they were deprived of access to some of the old periodicals.

Of course, with the almost total monopolization of the press by the Communist party, the Soviets needed access to some alternative media in order to communicate with the electorate. What is interesting is that their aim in those conflicts about the mass media was to create a propaganda system of their own. This is typical Soviet thinking. Thus, the Moscow legislature decided "to launch newspapers, radio and TV programs, other mass media, reflecting the position of the Moscow Soviet, to create its own printing base and an information-publishing center."[22]

It is a political tradition of a totalitarian country to form public opinion by means of fully controlled media. Politicians here do not think it sufficient to have attractive programs to draw people to their parties. They feel uncomfortable appealing to people through an independent press that they cannot manipulate. It is a Communist tradition, of course, but anti-Communists who came to power here act the same.

The Democratic Russia movement has offered to conduct a referendum on nationalization of party property, as though complex legal problems like these could be solved by a vote. There is legislation in the country that could provide a basis for their legal solution but, the opposition has preferred to use the issue as a trump card in its political game. The party had a lot of property, of course, but for its political opponents this is not just a matter of money but of discrediting their nemesis and directing the anger of the people, who feel they have been robbed, against it.

There was no referendum, but after the putsch in August 1991 the party was prohibited and its property taken over by the Russian government. It was done without any courts, by a presidential edict, as Vladimir Lenin handled matters in 1917. Lenin confiscated and nationalized property of private owners and Yeltsin did the same to the party estate. But Yeltsin avoided the verb *confiscate*; ownership was "transferred under the jurisdiction of the Russian government." In this country what are called "revolutionary justice" and "revolutionary expediency" are not solely the privilege of Bolsheviks.

With the declining influence of Communist ideology over public opinion and growing mistrust of its official organs, the party has launched quite a number of new publications. Many of them, such as the newspapers of the district party committees in Moscow, resembled small independent tabloids and were definitely intended to compete with the latter. They did not last long.

After the putsch, the major Communist newspaper, *Pravda*, was registered by its working collective as its founder. The editor-in-chief resigned and his former deputy took the post. According to some reports in the press, the newspaper was looking for a rich sponsor abroad. Robert Maxwell, who had had long contacts with the Communist leaders of the Soviet Union, was mentioned as a possible source of support but soon afterward he died.

Since the party was losing its political power, it tried to preserve its property by all means including the use of military force. In Riga in the autumn of 1990, special troops took control of the press building and held it for a while disrupting publication of newspapers. This occurred as the outcome of a conflict between the republican government, which refused to share press profits with CPSU and tried to establish its control over the publishing facilities, and the Communist leaders of Latvia who were submissive to Moscow. The government adopted a resolution, "About returning to the Latvian Republic an illegally expropriated newspaper-magazine publishing house." In response, the Central Committee of the Communist Party of the CPSU declared the publishing house its property.

Early in January 1991, internal troops seized the main publishing plant in Riga. Print workers announced a protest strike. The workers and editorial staff decided to halt work and to bring legal charges against those responsible for the occupation of the building rather than face direct confrontation with armed units by continuing to work at their jobs in the building.

At the same time, internal troops were used to take over and control the party buildings in Lithuania. The troops also took over the press building in Vilnius. The military used force to break into the building, and one of the warning shots fired into the air struck a worker. The workers were forced to leave the building.

Later in January, about twenty Soviet soldiers of the internal troops armed with automatic weapons, accompanied by two civilian representatives of the Lithuanian Communist party, took over the main newsprint warehouse in Vilnius. They were reportedly carrying out the March 28, 1990, resolution of the USSR Council of Ministers on protection of party property.

Direct military force to guard and secure party ownership was exceptional; various financial attempts were more typical.

The party was secretly taking care of its future. It did its best to preserve its capital, which would provide some financial stability that might help it to survive the political vicissitudes. It invested in many commercial banks and enterprises in the country and abroad. According to some reports, from early 1991 until the August putsch the party converted rubles into dollars through its joint ventures with foreign companies and transferred them to foreign banks, mostly through the KGB.[23]

Investigators from the General Procurator's Office of the Russian Republic who are trying to locate the bank accounts of the party here and abroad experience a number of problems. Many accounts were probably opened with false names. Besides, when the Russian investigators asked for help, the foreign bankers did not hurry to disclose real investors because the requests were not well enough supported from a legal point of view. And actually no court had ever determined that the bank accounts of the Communist party should be confiscated.

According to a member of the Commission of the Russian Supreme Soviet on the financial activities of the Communist party, Alexei Surkov, "Prosperity of hundreds of enterprises, dozens of banks, foreign companies founded on the capital of the CPSU, leads to the major conclusion: the underground Central Committee is acting.... Establishment of "new" pro-Communist parties could not do without its financial participation."[24]

There has been some fragmentary information about the party's hidden investments in the news media. The Leningrad Communist party organization has invested 400,000 rubles in a radio company.[25] *Sovetskaya Rossiya*, which was banned after the putsch, was restored by its "working collective" and a private businessman, Andrei Zavidiya. It was discovered that his company obtained 3 million rubles from the Central Committee of the Communist Party of Russia as a no-interest credit, although Zavidiya publicly denied getting any money from the party.

When the party was outlawed after the putsch, Zavidiya became one of the newspaper's founders and started supporting it. He was also a cofounder of the conservative newspaper *Den*. During the elections of 1991, Zavidiya was nominated for vice president with the right-winger Vladimir Zhirinovky, who ran for president against Boris Yeltsin.[26]

Zavidiya made it clear that his support of the *Sovetskaya Rossiya* was not going to be a charitable activity but would help his future political career:

I think, considering that I have saved the newspaper in a difficult moment, it will not refuse to publish my election program.... Journalists work quite free and experience no pressure. But further on they will certainly have

to choose: either full freedom or my financial support. And if I shall invest
my money, I shall correspondingly dictate some stipulations of my own.[27]

It is very probable that there are quite a few media in the country now
secretly supported by party capital but specific information about them
is not available. For instance, one might surmise that a new Russian-
language publication started in Byelorussiya early in 1991, *Slavyanskiye
vedomosti*, was sponsored by the Communist party. The first issue promoted unity of the Great Russian, White Russian, and Little Russian
peoples (in current parlance Russians, Belorussians, and Ukrainians) and
reportedly contained anti-Semitic material. It is printed by the facilities
of the Belorussian Communist party, but, in violation of the press law,
the founder of the paper has not been identified.

Two months after the putsch, the *Moscow news* wrote: "Today chau-
vinist newspapers and magazines are launched at unknown capitals even
more intensively than earlier; openly provocative radio stations are starting their broadcasting (and this business needs dozens of millions). The
Party money has started working."[28] There is definitely some money
secretly invested in the media by the Communist party—and probably a
lot. Nevertheless, there is too little factual evidence so far to support
such generalizations.

IDEOLOGICAL MANAGEMENT IS OUT OF FASHION;
ECONOMIC CONTROL WORKS INSTEAD

There are tremendous economic pressures on the print media. After
fighting for liberation from ideological control, neither editors nor journalists were actually ready to face the new realities that it brought.
Everything in this life must be paid for. The Communist party and Communist state supported the press that promoted their ideology. The press
did not have to think about efficient economic management or making a
profit. It was an ideological tool and it was treated as such.

When the Communist ideology collapsed with the disintegration of the
party, financial support for the press disappeared, too. The rules of the
game changed and the establishment press couldn't play anymore.

Of course, there were crucial factors outside the media field that influenced the press negatively; one was rising costs. But it is characteristic
that the democratic press that had fought successfully for its ideological
independence appealed to the government for financial support. It seems
that it is too difficult to be free. It is evident that the editors and journalists who appeal to the government to subsidize their newspapers do
not realize that they are putting themselves in a very vulnerable position
and risking their independence as a result.

The situation became critical by the middle of February 1992, when the largest newspapers in the country, *Komsomolskaya pravda* and *Trud*, did not appear for several days because of lack of newsprint. Probably this caused President Yeltsin to sign the long-awaited edict "About additional measures for legal and economic defense of periodical press and state book publishing."[29]

Through this edict, which claims to promote market economy, the government has restored fixed prices (lower than production costs) for 70 percent of the newsprint and other kinds of paper for printing and publishing in the country. It is aimed at guaranteeing supplies for state book publishing and "newspapers and magazines published according to programs approved by the Ministry of Press and Mass Information of the Russian Federation." Paper producers are prohibited from selling their products abroad before their contracts with the state are fulfilled.

The government supported press was not only guaranteed supplies but freed from deductions from their foreign currency revenues. Special funds to reimburse distribution and delivery costs were also provided "within the framework of subscription circulation."

The edict also ordered the creation of a program for the privatization of the distribution system. If it is fulfilled, it will be the first real step to demonopolization in this sphere.

The edict ordered the Ministries of Economics and of Finance to allocate means for the Ministry of the Press for 1992 to subsidize periodicals and socially meaningful literature (textbooks and books for children).

The establishment press was saved by Yeltsin's edict almost at the last moment, and the government has assumed an obligation to guarantee its survival at least until the end of 1992.

Is this a happy end? No, it isn't, and not just because the press has had to face all the same problems since 1992. By paying for newsprint and delivery, the government is obtaining an instrument for control that is no less powerful than the ideological dictates of the Communist party.

Not all the periodical publications are supported by these means, but only those included in "programs approved by the Ministry of the Press." The same is true of direct subsidies to the printed media: the ministry will decide to whom to give, how much to give, and whether to give at all. By saving the printed media at the expense of the state budget, the government is prolonging its control over them. The fourth branch of power cannot be independent if it is subsidized by the government.

Just several days after the edict had been published, it became evident that its signing did not ensure that its promises would be fulfilled. The government needed over 60 billion rubles to pay subsidies and 11.5 billion for the other expenses foreseen by the edict but the budget, which ran a deficit, did not have this money.

The paper mills refused to sell newsprint at fixed prices that would cause their bankruptcy. It costs fourteen thousand to fifteen thousand rubles to produce a ton of newsprint, whereas the edict fixes prices at four thousand rubles. Managers of the industry announced that not a single mill would sell newsprint at this price and the only result would be a further decrease in production. *Moskovsky komsomolets* reported that despite the edict its supplier sells newsprint for 13,000 rubles a ton plus 28 percent tax because of an increase in the price of raw materials and electricity.

The general situation in the field is unclear. Because of lack of raw materials, some mills use only a part of their capacity. But at the same time, according to sources in the paper industry, "talks about newsprint starvation do not correspond to the reality." A number of state publishing houses are in the business of reselling the paper that they get at state prices at market prices.[30] In 1992–1993 the trend continued: newsprint prices kept growing, and while the commodity was usually unavailable at fixed prices (even when the government tried to impose them) newsprint could always be bought at free market prices.

The general reaction in the media to the edict was far from unanimous enthusiasm. Establishment publications, like *Komsomolskaya pravda* and, *Izvestiya* seemed to be satisfied although some embarrassment could be perceived in their comments about the edict. The independent press was naturally critical of it. This edict was a real test for the press: what price is it ready to pay for its freedom—or for its survival? It appears that economic realities not political differences form the line that will separate independent media from those that agree to be managed.

This distinction has already become evident. While *Izvestiya* wrote about the "jealous outrage of the commercial press" provoked by Yeltsin's edict,[31] *Nezavisimaya gazeta* criticized the "official press," which is "stubbornly engaged in extortion of public means." It called the edict

> a result of hysterical lobbying activities of the mass official newspapers and magazines. The use of populist pressure that was developed in the years of "early glasnost"—when newspapers gained astronomical circulations by lowering prices and then acquired subsidies from the state budget by blackmailing the authorities with "the millions of readers"—turned out to be effective again.[32]

Commercial publications know for sure that they have nobody but their readers and advertisers to rely on. The establishment, or official, press looks for support from the authorities. Several days after publication of the edict, newspaper editors got together with the minister of press, Michail Poltoranin, to discuss how the edict would be implemented.

Shortly before that, he was promoted to the post of vice prime minister, while keeping his ministerial position. Reactions on the promotion were polarized: the official press interpreted it as a recognition of media power, whereas independent outlets considered it an award for taming the press.

This meeting of the press minister with the editors reminded many of the ones that Communist officials used to have with the media managers. The topic for discussion was new but all the participants were brought together essentially on the same old basis: recognition of an interrelationship and mutual dependence of the authorities and the media. In countries where the mass media are really independent, there is no need for gatherings like these.

Even the headline of the *Izvestiya* report of the meeting was eloquently illogical: THE "FOURTH POWER" MUST BECOME POWER.[33] If it must become one, then it is not yet a power. Nevertheless, the media pretend that they are, inculcating in the readership the notion that the press can be both supported by the government and independent of it. "A special sensitivity of the issue," *Izvestiya* wrote in the same article,

> is in the fact that although the mass press has lost in the transitional period its material independence, it does not wish to renounce its moral independence. But representatives of power institutions are not always ready to accept and understand the fact that it is natural for the press to criticize the government although it has allocated money for the media.

Those complaints by the newspaper sound like a new generation of propaganda. In the time of Communist rule, the press pretended that it was free of ideological pressures. Now it pretends that it can be free of the pressures of the state while it lives on government subsidies, trying to do something that is not easy according to a Russian proverb: to preserve innocence and to acquire capital. Maybe there are calculating people able to do so (probably not) but certainly not the mass media.

Speaking before the editors as their generous sponsor, Poltoranin complained about how difficult it was for him to lobby for the edict among the bureaucrats in the Russian government. He managed to get lots of signatures to support the draft and help it pass. Nevertheless, the newspaper wrote, "he did not exclude a potential possibility to mobilize journalists 'to influence' some Russian bureaucrats if it will be necessary."

Evidently, nobody in the audience remembered that they represent "independent" media and nobody questioned the right of a government official to "mobilize" them. Maybe they really flatter themselves that they represent some "power," but they know certainly that there are powers much stronger than they and they must take this reality into consideration. Capital is apparently more important than innocence.

In this particular discussion, the concrete problem of the relationship between the government, and the media was discussed and the press was ready to use its might to lobby publicly for its own cause. But there is no doubt that the subsidized media can be easily manipulated in other cases of differences and conflicts, too, and they will surely speak for the government. The fact that the establishment press still considers itself an entity, not a number of independent outlets, in terms of ideology, management, and organization makes this manipulation even easier.

Instead of trying to be different and independent from each other, competing media look for common grounds. The time of tough market competition has come but the official newspapers still attempt to solve their problems through collective effort. It would not be so bad if they used economic means, say, some kind of joint operation agreement. But they unite not to solve their problems together but to press the government to solve them.

At the meeting with Poltoranin, *Izvestiya* wrote that the editors managed "to work out a common point of view on many not only tactical but also strategic issues." The fact that they have the same problems, "enables them to form a united policy with respect to the other three institutions of power—legislative, executive, and judicial."

Izvestiya correspondent Irina Demchenko has interpreted this agreement to mean that, even if the managers of the mass media have not yet perceived themselves to be a "fourth power," they are definitely moving in this direction.[34]

Another *Izvestiya* commentator, Nikolai Andreyev, excused government interference in the mass media, justifying a request by Vice Prime Minister Gennady Burbulis to the mass media "to provide ideological support for the Russian government." Yes, admits Andreyev, this requirement is very close to what Lenin demanded from the press—to be a mouthpiece and an instrument of the Communist party. Independence, of course, is an ideal for the media, the journalist comments, but in practice not everything is as simple as it is in theory.[35]

It appears that all this justification of media dependence on the authorities and lack of freedom of the press was presented to the reader mainly with one goal in mind. In late 1991, early 1992 *Izvestiya* became not only very loyal to the Russian government but an unreserved and energetic supporter of all its actions. Formally, there were no special ties between the two, but the newspaper's biased coverage made a thoughtful observer wonder what might prompt such excessive allegiance.

Evidently, many readers wondered about it, too.

> In the last time, Andreyev recognized, people around came to a conviction quite unexpectedly for us, that our newspaper "has been sold to the Russian government," that it stands on a pro-Russian position. Well, first, we have got no money from Russia, we have no privileges. We do not demand from anybody and can not demand any advantages in comparison to the other press outlets.[36]

Statements like that will hardly help the newspaper to cleanse its reputation. Of course, nobody has ever formally claimed that *Izvestiya* was "bought" by the Russian government. But there are things that remain unclear to the public. One of them is, of course, the unlimited loyalty; the other is the fact that unlike all the other central newspapers of the former Soviet Union, *Izvestiya* does not seem to experience painful problems with paper supplies, finance, and so on. It is being published regularly, without interruption, in full quantities. Why? Or, in other words, who pays? The question is still open. And so long as there is no direct answer to it, strong suspicions about *Izvestiya*'s hidden supporter and skepticism about its independence will remain.

Rossiiskaya gazeta in the issue of February 17, 1993 has offered its explanation of the loyalty of *Izvestiya* to the Russian president and government. It sounds cynical, but in today's Russia it is quite realistic. It was a matter of redistribution of state property. The newspaper unreservedly supported the executive branch because its management hoped in this turmoil to take over the entire publishing house Izvestiya. It didn't go through, but at least the newspaper was granted a building that belonged to Izvestia publishing house. The publishing house protested the decision as a violation of its rights, but by spring 1993 there was no final decision on the case.

The Russian media are by no means unique in the former Soviet Union in terms of their concept of media independence. The chief editors of Kazahstan republican newspapers warned President Nazarbaev that their papers might have to shut down since the republican Ministry of Communications has sharply increased the price of paper and postal delivery. Publishers could no longer make ends meet and wanted Nazarbaev to intervene with the Ministry.[37]

Will a press that has a very distorted idea of what "the fourth branch of government" really means be able to survive in a democratic society based on a market economy? The question is rhetorical. The media have been working hard to destroy the Communist system of power. And now that it has been demolished they are trying to prolong their own existence but they do it in vain. They are only parts of the old system and they are doomed to disappear with it. They will live only for as long as the post-Communist governments extend their lifetime by financial injections.

The edict does not guarantee equal support to all the printed press. The unfavored publications will have a difficult time paying market prices for newsprint and distribution without subsidies. They will learn to do business by relying on only themselves. Not all of them will survive but it is here that a really independent press free not only of ideological pressures but also of the government economic control will emerge.

As to the establishment media, it turned out to be much easier for them to change their way of thinking (from Communist to anti-Communist) than to change their methods of existence. Now they keep exploiting their declining popularity. For many decades they had no competition in their respective areas and as a result they gained millions of readers. But a habit cannot last forever. For as long as they remain subservient to the government, their popularity will fall while the independent media gain readers. The independents will develop into the fourth branch of government.

The events in the spring of 1992 support this prediction. The most recent attempt to solve economic problems by means of edicts and decrees failed again, as did so many in the course of the Soviet history. Early in March 1992 *Pressa* publishing house reported that *Pravda, Komsomolskaya pravda, Selskaya zhizn, Rabochaya tribuna,* and other dailies must be limited to only three issues a week, at least for a while. Because of sharp increase in the prices of newsprint, production, and delivery, the newspapers had spent all the money they received for annual subscriptions by the end of February 1992. Advertising revenues turned out to be much lower than expected. The director of *Pressa,* Viacheslav Leontiev, did not exclude the possibility that the number of issues would fall to one a week. The situation of *Pravda* was the worst. To provide for publication at least three times a week, it had to apply for a loan. It also appealed to its readers for financial support. The editorial board considered publication of a four page weekly instead of a daily.[38]

The worst prognosis for the future of *Pravda* came true much sooner than might be expected. In the middle of March 1992 it suspended publication for a week, it was officially announced; in fact, the prospect of its publishing in the future was quite unclear.

It is no wonder that *Pravda* was the first victim of the new economic situation. It happened of course because it was a cornerstone of the collapsed system and could not outlast it. Equally important, it had put itself in disrepute by its enthusiastic support of the August putsch. It was not the only supporter but it was the loudest.

It was reported that *Pravda* would resume publication after it paid its debt to the publisher. It was also expected that two other former Communist party newspapers, *Sovetskaya Rossiya* and *Rabochaya tribuna* would fold too.[39]

Although *Pravda* in Moscow has suspended publication (for a while) its offspring, *Novaya pravda* (*Digest of the Russian press*), appeared in Paris, edited by a long-time *Pravda* correspondent in France, Vladimir Bolshakov. The newspaper was supposed to be published twice a month and contain articles from *Pravda, Selskaya zhizn, Komsomolskaya pravda, Rabochaya tribuna,* and other newspapers published by the Pressa publishing house.

Novaya pravda is rather expensive: fifteen franks. Its circulation is thirty thousand copies. The newcomer has been promoted by an organ of the Communist party of France, *Humanité,* which called upon its readers to buy the new publication, because "it is an excellent way to get information and simultaneously to help *Pravda*." It could get some money for the parent publication if it really sold, but according to the Paris correspondent of *Nezavisimaya gazeta*, it did not. Eight out of ten Paris newsstands he examined did not sell a single copy.[40]

This new enterprise again attracted the attention of the public to the undercover operations of the Communist party of the Soviet Union with foreign currency. For a long time, many foreign Communist parties as well as their publications were financed from the USSR. In the last period of the Soviet Union when the party was gradually losing power, it transferred abroad large volumes of foreign currency for its own use.

Now that *Novaya pravda* has begun, the first question is who finances the new enterprise. Can a newspaper that is almost bankrupt do that? Or the party, which has been prohibited? The venture will be a new stimulus for discussion of Communist party capital secretly transferred abroad to foreign banks in anonymous accounts.

But a more general question, not only of financial but of political importance, may be the real goal of an enterprise like this: is the purpose to make money for *Pravda* or is its wider aim to restore the Communist system in this country? The fact that the venture is so far from here does not make much difference. On the contrary, Bolsheviks had considerable expertise in publishing their newspapers abroad and directing and organizing revolutionary movements by leaders who lived in foreign countries over long periods.

Of course, restoration of Communism is not an immediate danger now. Nevertheless, all the attempts of the ideological nomenklatura to create its support stations abroad should be watched carefully.

Although the situation of spring 1992 looked almost a catastrophe, most of the press, including Communist, still survived. Actually, the entire economy was in more or less the same situation at that time, after the policy of "shock therapy" was started at the beginning of the year. It took time to adapt to it. Some newspapers obtained government subsidies. Criteria for their distribution has never been made quite clear, and this has provided opportunity for mismanagement of the subsidies: most went to government supporters. Formally all the newspapers are equal, but in fact, according to Orwellian logic, "some newspapers are more equal than others." Those "others" had to find private donors, or diversify their activities, or to find some other additional sources of income. Thus *Nezavisimaya gazeta* claims that it does not get any government subsidies, and while the newspaper itself loses money, the company makes ends meet with book publishing and selling information from its news agency. Lack of financial support forced some opposition dailies to cut down the number of issues as well as the number of pages.

Fifty-one percent of *Pravda* was bought by a Greek publisher, provoking speculations in the press that the money invested was part of funds hidden abroad by the Communist Party. But nothing was officially proved. *Rabochaya tribuna* has among its co-founders the federation of independent trade unions and the Russian union of industrialists and entrepreneurs, who evidently support it. *Sovetskaya Rossiya* is in part subsidized by private capital, but does not get enough funding to publish more than three 4-page issues a week. According to the above mentioned results of subscription for 1993 these Communist newspapers, although their circulations are lower than those of *Izvestiya* or *Komsomolskaya pravda*, lost a smaller percentage of their readers than the papers supporting Yeltsin and his government.

One reason is evident and external to the media: dissatisfaction with a government that is unable to improve the economy, the declining level of life—in a word, disillusion with the present powers. The rising prices of newspapers played their role in this process, too.

Another reason is that by their unlimited and uncritical support of the government the democratic media ruined the image of the independent press they tried to create for themselves. It was anti-Communist propaganda, but of typically Communist style. The press did not do much good for the government, because the efforts to manipulate public opinion were too obvious. But what is more important for the press itself is that its integrity was violated. People started questioning press honesty and trustworthiness. The press is losing readers because it is losing their trust.

NOTES

1. *Lenin Anthology*, ed. Robert Tucker. W. W. Norton & Company, N.Y., 1975, p. 149.

2. Ibid., p. 150.

3. Nikolai Fyodorov. Still trying to influence. *Moscow News*, No. 11, 1990, p. 14.

4. The Law of the Union of the Soviet Socialist Republics on the Press and Other Mass Media (in Russian). *Zhournalist*, No. 8, 1990, p. 12–16.

5. *Argumenti i fakti*, No. 13, 1991, p. 7.

6. Vera Tolz, Adoption of the Press Law: A New Situation for the Soviet Media? Report on the USSR. Radio Liberty. July 6, 1990, p.11.

7. Vladimir Vigilyansky, An open letter to the members of the working collective of the magazine *Ogonyok*. *Stolitsa*, No. 41–42, 1991, p. 68.

8. Ibid., p. 70.

9. A commentator of *Stolitsa* Michail Pozdnjaev talks to the author of the "Open letter," former member of the editorial board of "Ogonyok" Vladimir Vigilyansky. *Stolitsa*, No. 41–42, 1991, p. 70–74.

10. *Izvestiya*, August 1, 1990; July 26, 1990; *Literaturnaya gazeta*, July 11, 1990.

11. *Los Angeles Times*, January 31, 1991.

12. A. Illesh, V. Rudnev, "Censorship lifted, censors remain. An attempt of a review of a book on state secrets." *Izvestiya*, October 9, 1990.

13. Ibid.

14. "There is no censorship, but secrets remain." An interview by the head of the Chief Administration for the Protection of State Secrets in the Press and Other Mass Media of the USSR V. A. Boldirev. *Izvestiya*, July 26, 1990.

15. Vitaly Tretyakov, "Independence is our style." *Nezavisimaya gazeta*, April 4, 1991.

16. *Radio Free Europe/Radio Liberty Daily Report*, February 20, 1991.

17. *Izvestiya*, February 16, 1991; *Radio Free Europe/Radio Liberty Daily Report*, February 1, 1991.

18. *Moscow news*, No. 43, 1990, p. 14. *Kuryer*, No. 2, July 1990, p. 2. *Nezavisimaya gazeta*, August 8, 1991. *Rossiya*, No. 29, 1991, p. 4.

19. *Moskovsky komsomolets*, August 2, 1990.

20. *Moscow news*, No. 43, 1990, p. 14.

21. *Radio Free Europe/Radio Liberty Daily Report*, February 4, 1991.

22. *Izvestiya*, May 30, 1990.

23. *Moscow news*, No. 41, 1991, p. 8.

24. *Komsomolskaya pravda*, December 21, 1991.

25. *Rossiya*, No. 29, 1991, p. 4.

26. *Commersant*, No. 36, 1991, p. 3. *Moscow news*, No. 36, 1991, p. 4; No. 49, 1991, p. 11. *Komsomolskaya pravda*, October 8, 1991.

27. *Komsomolskaya pravda*, September 28, 1991.

28. *Moscow news*, No. 41, 1991, p. 8.

29. *Komsomolskaya pravda*, February 22, 1992; *Nezavisimaya gazeta*, February 22, 1992.

30. *Nezavisimaya gazeta*, February 29, 1992.

31. *Izvestiya*, February 26, 1992.

32. *Nezavisimaya gazeta*, February 22, 1992.

33. *Izvestiya*, February 26, 1992.

34. Ibid.

35. *Izvestiya*, March 11, 1992.

36. Ibid.

37. *Izvestiya*, January 26, 1991.

38. *Moscovsky komsomolets*, March 4, 1992.

39. *Nezavisimaya gazeta*, March 14, 1992.

40. *Nezavisimaya gazeta*, March 17, 1992.

3

A GAME WITHOUT RULES: FIGHT FOR CONTROL OVER TV

NO PROPAGANDA, JUST CONVICTION

Until the collapse of the Union, the fight for television had several dimensions. It was conducted between the central authorities and the republics, between the Communist party and the newly emerging political forces, and, of course, within the television organization itself—not just between journalists and management (and among journalists, too, no doubt), but people at the top of the Gosteleradio.

They could be roughly divided into two groups: professionals and cadre recruited from the party nomenklatura. The latter are not experts in the field but they are usually the bosses and have the final say in decision making. As everywhere in the country, it is through these people that the party apparat has pursued its politics. As a rule, they do not need direct orders and even less everyday guidance—they are reliable; they can be trusted. But professionals naturally are not happy about having such managers and so misunderstanding and tension are inevitable.

One might argue that once the separation of the state and the party had been declared by the highest level of power in the country and the article of the Constitution that used to provide for the leading role of the party in society had been altered, the situation would be different. It might seem so but it wasn't. For me, the most shocking (although I cannot say unexpected) proof appeared during the summer of 1990, when several high-ranking officials of the Central Committee (it was announced publicly that its staff was being reduced) were quietly moved to the top of Gosteleradio—at a time when the broadcasting organization was itself about to face reorganization and dismissals.

The aim of this cadre shift was clearly not only to provide comfortable places for the people from the party apparat (although it was important and the system always did its best to secure the future of those who served it) but also to preserve Communist party control over TV by keeping trustworthy personnel in important positions. The party was losing more and more ground, but it was clinging to power and was fighting strongly to preserve its domain. Television with its command over public opinion was one of the most sensitive points in this fight, and prolonging control over it was crucial.

What made opposition to radical changes in the establishment even stronger were the events in Eastern Europe in the late 1980s, including those in the mass media. These developments indicated very impressively and convincingly what could happen to apparatchiks or sometimes even rank and file Communists (especially if they occupied positions that allowed them to influence public opinion) when new political forces came to power. It's worth remembering that, however peaceful the 1989 revolution in Czechoslovakia was, dismissals of Communists from the national television soon followed.

New political realities call for a reconsideration of the mass media's role in society. While the new forces that emerged on the scene pushed for a marketplace of ideas, representatives of the establishment resisted any serious revision of the traditional role of the media as an element of the party-government structure and a tool of its power. They tried to reformulate the old Lenin principles that were at the core of the obsolete ideological system and adapt them to the new situation. According to those principles, the media had to be instrumental in party politics; their three major functions were propaganda, so-called agitation (convincing people to take certain actions, to participate in certain political campaigns), and organization. Information as such was far from the first priority; it was not even mentioned in the list of the most important roles.

As the party and state authorities in the period of perestroika saw it, the new version of the role of the media was formulated most explicitly by Michail Nenashev, chairman of Gosteleradio till autumn 1990, when a conservative shift in Soviet politics began. Nenashev published in *Pravda* a long article titled "Television: time of changes," in which he specified the three major functions of TV at that time: "to inform, to convince, and to comfort."[1]

At last there was official recognition that the mass information media must first of all inform, not distribute propaganda. It really appeared to be an indication of the era of glasnost that everyone would be happy to embrace. But the Gosteleradio chairman did not go so far as to acknowledge that entertainment is one of the most important functions of the media as is recognized to be everywhere else. Although entertainment always existed in one form or another, it was officially regarded with definite suspicion as unworthy second-rate stuff: it was not in the same class as serious propaganda programming, which was always welcome regardless of whether people watched it or not.

And what did it mean "to convince"? It sounded like a slightly veiled euphemism for propagandizing. Nenashev had actually confirmed it: "Television must not only inform, but also convince, form optimism and trust for the politics of the party and the state."[2]

The question is how this notion corresponds with the function of informing people, which supposes a certain degree of objectivity. This is an especially delicate question for the Soviet media, which have never had a tradition of a distinct separation of news from opinion and there has always been a strong emphasis on propaganda at the expense of information. Besides, news was also viewed and used as an instrument of propaganda. Evidently things did not change much. "In practice, Nenashev admitted in one of his interviews, we not only inform a person, but deliberately influence his consciousness."[3]

Discussing the function of convincing people, Nenashev strongly emphasized "the issue of the party" among the topics that do not get enough coverage on TV (although it was state, rather than party, TV and the leading role of the CPSU was no longer specified in the Constitution). He condemned "a definite sliding of television both at the center and on the local level from the party-mindedness positions," that, he continued, "can't help causing our serious anxiety and discontent."[4]

Again, I must remind you that this is the working principle of the head of the only television system in a supposedly pluralistic society. The last problem but not the least was the fact that the Gosteleradio chairman was at the same time a member of the Central Committee of the Communist party.

The third major role of TV that Nenashev listed deserves special attention. We should consider both the way the task was justified and the methods of its implementation in the everyday work of the Soviet television. As to the practical incentives for this role, Nenashev put it this way:

> Now, when the situation in our country is very complicated, when we are forced to solve simultaneously a huge number of difficult problems, we ought not only to influence people's consciousness, to convince them, but at the same time to try to bring a definite balance into the moral atmosphere of the society. To be, if you like, confessors, to comfort people, to support their optimism and trust.[5]

In another article, published half year later, Nenashev denounced the critical mood that dominated the media: "I think by those means we do not bring the Soviet people optimism, confidence in the success of the large matter started in April 1985."[6]

Supporting people's optimism in the time of a full-fledged political and economic crisis is an extremely difficult task. Although Communist dogmas or, at least, their practical implementation failed, the documents of the party until its collapse kept insisting on "the Socialist choice and the Communist perspective" for the country. During the last years of the Soviet Union the official mass propaganda, although it already hesitated to use the old ideological clichés, was unable to develop any attractive new ideas to offer the public to inspire it.

Nevertheless, according to Nenashev, optimism had to be promoted. The one thing that might achieve that end would be improving the situation in the country. But this of course was beyond the competence of Gosteleradio. It found no other way to encourage optimism but to present faith healers (introduced as psychotherapists), who claimed not only to comfort people but to cure their ailments—instantly and over the airwaves.

In spite of the protests of many medical professionals, these people obtained access to a multimillion viewer audience and had regular time in the schedule for a while. These anti-intellectual medieval performances distributed by means of modern electronic media attracted lots of people who were strongly inclined to believe in miracles.

There could be no more frightening indication of the depth of the moral degradation of the society. Historical analogies often help us understand the present: the one that many people think of in this case is really depressing. The late 1980s and early 1990s situation as a whole and particularly the appeal to blind trust rather than reason reminds one of the eve of the Bolshevik revolution, when another miracle worker, a "saintly old man," Grigory Rasputin, actually ruled the country. Of course, he influenced only the rulers. These faith healers with modern communications appealed to the millions.

Of course, every comparison leaves much to be desired. However, the fact that the Communist leaders (the Gosteleradio officials acted on their behalf) approved the appearance of faith healers on national TV to comfort the demoralized public revealed the helplessness of the authorities in dealing with the country's problems, as well as their lack of both intellectual arguments and moral values.

And it was not only faith healers to whom the authorities appealed for help in managing public opinion. They also provided air time for representatives of the long neglected and repressed Russian Orthodox Church (but none of the other religions that are widely practiced in the country), trying to calm irritated, dissatisfied people to keep them under control. The goal may have been achieved to some extent for a while, but nevertheless the method was inappropriate. By choosing representatives of one religion and ignoring others, television created tension and exasperation in segments of society and violated the principle of separation of church and state.

A number of religious leaders became very active in politics during perestroika; some were elected people's deputies (members of legislatures at different levels). The state, which had long ignored or persecuted religious leaders, turned to them for support in this period of instability and turmoil. This alliance of church and state is one of the dangers that complicated the creation of democracy in our society.

Wide criticism of the existing TV structure and claims of the new political forces to some part of it probably Forced Michail Nenashev to hold official press conferences periodically—an unprecedented act. At his first conference, Nenashev in response to those who asked to share the TV with the existing powers blatantly proclaimed the aims of the system he headed: "The state television has the right to existence and it must exist in that form in which it exists now," he said. "We defend the interests of the state, the interests of the country. We are the state television, financed and managed by the government."[7]

In one interview, Nenashev stressed the same point: "Our television is a state, Soviet, socialist one, whether anybody likes it or not . . . . The task of television is to defend perestroika from pressures both from the right and from the left."[8]

The underlying assumption of these statements is that all political forces except the Communist party should seek alternative television channels, if and when they are available. In July 1990, this idea was developed in a presidential decree.

When the Gosteleradio chairman was asked whether television would aid the emergence of a multiparty system, he explained that prospects for its development "do not depend on whether the Central Committee of the Communist party or television will support it." He pointed out that it is "a natural process," that "can not be imposed from the top. Certain democratic conditions must mellow. We do not have them so far," he said, referring to the fact that until autumn 1990 the country had no law pertaining to political movements and organizations. At the time of the interview, the law was being drafted. Besides, Nenashev said, "the society itself is not ready yet; all the necessary democratic conditions for appearance of those parties and movements have not been created."[9]

Nenashev's remarks were rather awkward because a number of parties had already come into being and new ones continued to emerge, ignoring Nenashev's assertion that it was not yet time for their birth.

And as far as the new parties' access to the mass media is concerned, Nenashev insisted that they should "travel their road from the very beginning, starting with the press, and later on, maybe on a cooperative basis, to arrange radio and television studios."[10]

There can be no doubt that on its way to power the Communist party did "travel its road from the very beginning." But one of the actions it took soon after the revolution (and it was a milestone on this road that determined the major direction of development for the next seventy years) was to outlaw other parties and ban their newspapers. Not all new parties that came into being recently, but some of them, consider themselves descendents of those that were prohibited. Asking them "to travel their road from the very beginning" did not seem to be very fair. The reemergence of a multi-party system demanded that the Communist party pay its historical debts. But no one had any illusions that it ever would.

In response to those who criticized TV, Nenashev insisted (and he was apparently right) that "television cannot be better than life."[11] It may be more correct to say that TV cannot be better than the system in which it operates. It is no wonder that the television monopoly was so strictly guarded: denouncing it is a challenge to the system itself. And if television cannot be better than the system, then the system, which runs TV, must be changed first. That would create among other things, radical changes in TV's structure, as well. Attempts to reform the system were widespread and evident, and so was stubborn opposition to change.

WHERE THE POWER IS: A PROJECTION
ON THE TV SCREEN

Under perestroika in the Soviet Union, the famous slogan "All the power to the Soviets" that was the banner of the Bolshevik Revolution became popular again, though its connotation was quite different. It didn't mean to seize power by overthrowning the legitimate government by force, but rather to defeat the Communist party–dominated structures with democratically elected institutions and to liberalize the country. But a slogan is one thing and real life another. The situation on Soviet TV gave a clear answer to the question of where the real power lay, regardless of the slogans proclaimed.

One of the most important achievements of glasnost is that it made politics public, at least to a substantial degree. As a result, people could witness events and clashes that previously would have never become known or officially admitted and discussed. At best they might have become the talk of the town. The same was true of the situation on television.

The most important step toward glasnost on television and in politics came about in 1989 with live broadcasts of the first Congress of People's Deputies, formed as a result of the free elections. The broadcasts unmasked personalities on the political stage and made immediately evident who was who in policy and what the balance of forces was in the fight for power that was taking place.

But at the same time, it quickly and inevitably provoked appeals—not from the audience, but from some individuals inside the lawmaking body itself—to stop the broadcasts. This first sip of revitalizing freedom made the public enthusiastic, but to the people whose power was challenged it tasted like poison.

And that was just the beginning. From that time whenever a major political event such as a party congress or a parliamentary session was to take place, the question of broadcasting it provoked sharp discussions: should it be live or taped, full or edited? Broadcasts were never live, with the exception of Gorbachev's speeches; the official reasoning was that in the daytime people should work, not watch TV. Editing was not very extensive, but did center on vital points; that's why information about cuts was inevitably leaked to the press and became a subject of public discussion.

Thus, extracts were taken from the taped broadcast of a Supreme Soviet session that discussed the fate of two of its members, Gdlian and Ivanov. Criminal investigators by occupation, they claimed that they revealed corruption at the highest level of the state and party management. The general prosecutor, who tried to stop them in order to defend the reputation of the old cadre, demanded that the Parliament would grant him permission to dismiss the investigators from the Procuracy. Gdlian and Ivanov had wide popular support and they were elected deputies. It was natural that the hearings attracted much attention throughout the country. TV viewers, who had already had some negative experiences, demanded that the session be fully televised and the chairman of the Supreme Soviet, Anatoly Lukyanov, promised to do so.

But the TV audience never saw that it took several ballots (the parliament had to vote five times on the same point), while the wording and packaging of this painful issue were altered, for the leaders of the Supreme Soviet to force the adoption of the resolution they liked. Those maneuvers of the leaders and their manipulation by the members' vote not only were unethical but involved a number of violations of parliamentary rules.

In spite of all the promises, extracts were made from the tape, "distorting the entire impression of the procedure of the parliamentary hearings," *Komsomolskaya pravda* wrote.[12] In spite of the censorship of the tape, the truth was revealed, adding to public distrust of the powers and their media.

At a meeting with Michail Gorbachev, then the secretary general of the CPSU, and the secretaries of local party committees that took place during the 28th Congress of the CPSU, the audience demanded that television cameras be removed from the hall. They were not because

Gorbachev had to speak. But the debate was so ridiculous that even a very loyal Communist newspaper, *Rabochaya tribuna (Workers' tribune)*, published by the Central Committee of the party, criticized the incident.[13] The harsh discussion was, of course, cut out of the tape that aired later.

Both the incident and the fact that it was not broadcast again revealed the limits of glasnost. They were vague and uncertain and could easily be constricted. This was especially true with respect to the organization that for decades had been the only real power in the country and under perestrioka was desperately fighting to preserve its might, privileges, and prestige—namely the Communist party, and its functionaries.

National TV heavily censored speeches to the Congresses of People's Deputies that were taped and shown by the second channel of Soviet television. All criticism of Gorbachev from the December 18, 1990, speech of Nicolai Travkin, leader of the Democratic party of Russia, had been cut. Travkin said the only part of Gorbachev's speech that had any relevance to the needs of ordinary people was his call for a fight against pornography.[14]

Incidents like these proved (if anyone needed such proof) that glasnost and freedom of the press were not the same thing. The limits of glasnost were determined from the top and during the periods when political struggle intensified and officialdom felt its power threatened the authorities readily narrowed those limits.

The fight for television took place at all levels of power. Long-lasting taboos collapsed. Under the Soviet system, a correspondent of a national newspaper or TV in a republic was considered a representative of a central body and was guaranteed some kind of protection. He or she was entitled to criticize local institutions.

Perestroika and glasnost made those relationships more complicated. The drive of republics and national territories for sovereignty, on the one hand, and the Center's effort to keep them together, on the other, inevitably generated conflicts. Journalists who represented the national media found themselves caught in the cross fire: the editors of the central media, to whom they were subordinate, and the local authorities where they worked and lived. In the new situation, it became very possible that the Center would support loyal local authorities rather than the journalists. They provided the base for the pyramid of power, not the media people. Thus, the methods of the gatekeepers of the national TV were determined primarily by the idea of the preservation of the Soviet Union as an entity.

In September 1990, the Gosteleradio correspondent in the Checheno-Ingush autonomous republic, Tamara Alieva, reported on national TV that the session of the republican Supreme Soviet was not properly broadcast by local TV. As she commented, the coverage was limited to several short pieces of the tape, the sessions took place behind closed doors, and journalists' access to the event was strictly limited.

The official reaction to the report in the republican capital Grozni was immediate and adverse. The Presidium of the Supreme Soviet of the republic gathered for an urgent meeting and the protest was delivered to Moscow. Gosteleradio responded on the same day: a telephone call from them informed Alieva that the TV bureau in Grozni was closed.[15]

But that was not the end of the incident. On two subsequent days, the national evening news program, "Vremya", broadcast a comment on Alieva's report by the chairman of the Checheno-Ingush Supreme Soviet, Zavgaev, who was also the first secretary of the republican party committee. He blamed Alieva for overstatements and described to the multimillion all-union TV audience how democratic the session that she criticized really was. The first deputy chairman of Gosteleradio, Pyotr Reshetov, failed to explain to the correspondent of *Moscow news* exactly what Alieva's mistakes were, if any, because nobody ever bothered to check the facts. But, the official said, he could not ignore the opinion "of a respectable man, Zavgaev."[16]

Nevertheless, in our time, blatant manifestations of dictatorial power and violation of glasnost are not so typical. But restraint of the press and censorship of information still exist, although probably not in such an awkward way. It is more evident and more harmful in the state monopoly TV structure than in the printed media, which are visibly evident and rapidly becoming diversified.

The situation in the Checheno-Ingush republic was not the most representative of a time when national units within the Soviet Union were widely pushing for independence. The ethnic movement in the republic was not strong enough to claim power then, unlike those in all union republics and some of the autonomous republics. Although they remained in powerful positions, the local oldliners did not have popular support and, in any conflict such as control over the media, they needed to apply for support from far-away Moscow because that was the only place where they could find it. Later the strong nationalist leader General Dudayev took over the Communist leadership of the autonomous republic.

More typical was the opposition of a republican government to the central authorities, including those supervising television. The Baltic republics were the first to declare their television independent of Gosteleradio. The pattern was followed by others.

Tensions between the republics and the Center were sometimes revealed in people's attitudes to national television. One of the episodes of the evening news program "Vremya" on June 28, 1990, was a report from Moldavia. When a correspondent of Gosteleradio, Ivan Petkov, asked a local citizen a question beginning "What would you say about...," the answer was, "I shall say, Down with Petkov."

Of course it was an achievement of glasnost that the episode was aired at all. But at the same time the very situation inevitably raised the question of why Gosteleradio kept in the republic a correspondent to whom the local people's attitude was, to put it mildly, unfriendly. And why they disliked him so much.

The answer was obvious: the journalist, whatever his professional and personal characteristics, was responsible to the authorities in Moscow not the local audience. People in the republic must have perceived him not just as a correspondent but as a symbol of the central power that they wanted to get rid of.

Behind every such conflict there was usually a long-time dissatisfaction among the local people with the All-Union authorities and the coverage of the republic's problems in the national media. And this was surely not the only conflict of this kind although not all of them were publicized. Among those widely discussed, was a confrontation between a *Pravda* correspondent in the Western Ukraine and the local population and the authorities.

The conflict Ivan Petkov faced in Moldova was quite different from the one Alieva experienced in the Checheno-Ingush republic. He opposed local people but satisfied the authorities and his job was safe. Alieva did the opposite and was dismissed. Petkov is not to be blamed specifically; he is just an example. In fact, he is typical of the journalistic culture that prevailed in the Soviet Union for decades.

The first and chief rule of survival in the media (both for the institution and for individuals) was to please the bosses, not the public. Of course bosses are important everywhere but in other countries the public also matters. When young journalists, starting their professional careers, tried to refer to the audience in their discussions with editors, they were taught: you do not work for the audience; you work for Staraya ploschad ("Old Square": the address of the Central Committee of the Communist party).

A Ukrainian television journalist, V. Scherbachev, advocating the cause of alternative television, stressed that it would serve the interests of the viewer better. "To be honest," he wrote, "we forget about him, considering the opinions of our superintendents to be more important for our work."[17]

However unbelievable it may sound now, when changes in our lives are so rapid and obvious, this mentality still prevails among the Gosteleradio officials. When in August 1990 the present author interviewed First Deputy Chairman Pyotr Reshetov, said of the audience: "If you want to listen, listen; if you do not want, do not listen. I do not worry about it." And indeed, what was there to worry about, as long as the state monopoly prevailed?

The attitude to the public in the printed media is different now that many alternative newspapers and magazines have appeared, providing choices for readers and threatening circulations of the official publications (all of which have been rapidly declining). In television a viewer has nothing to select from, and declarations of republican TV independence, however important they may be to national identity and self-esteem, do not create any additional or alternative programming either.

Conflicts of interest between the public and the rulers exist in any political system, but when the media structure is diversified, they are likely to be solved more equitably. In the Soviet Union, sharp disagreements between the audiences and the TV establishment will continue as long as the state controls the broadcasting system and the public will always be the loser.

By a coincidence that appears to be significant, on the same day that the "Vremya" program was broadcast, the press reported that Moldova eliminated the republican committee for television and radio and replaced it with a national television and radio broadcasting system for Moldova. There were several variations of organization under discussion, and the one approved by the republican Supreme Soviet was designed to make it as independent of any official body, government or parliament, as possible. The latter was given only one right—to appoint the general director.[18]

Several new departments that had no analogues in the previous structure were created in the new organization: advertising, foreign relations (which used to be a function of Gosteleradio), and others. They were supposed to provide for the accountability of the entire system. The system was also depoliticized, meaning that no parties or other political organizations were allowed to have their cells on radio and TV. The national television and radio also planned to station its correspondents abroad (previously only Gosteleradio had foreign correspondents) and to produce TV programs jointly with neighboring countries.

As far as the new organization's relationship with Gosteleradio was concerned, it was not one of supervisor and subordinate, as it used to be, but of equal partners. They planned to have a common technical policy, copyright regulations, and professional training system. Moldova became the first republic not only to proclaim its TV independent but to adopt a law providing for the development of a new structure. It also precisely separated functions that the republic considered its sole responsibility from those it delegated to the Center or shared with it.

The other republics certainly followed suit in one form or another. But one republic had nothing it could declare independent because it did not have a republican channel—Russia. Until recently it was taken for granted that the national channels originating from Moscow serve Russia, too. But when the republic became truly independent of the central legislature, as well as the government, it recognized that its interests were different from and sometimes opposite to those of the All-Union authorities. In this situation, lack of direct access to the airwaves could no longer be tolerated.

Late in 1990, Gorbachev and Yeltsin agreed "in principle" to set up a radio and TV company for the RSFSR. But implementing the agreement was not an easy task. When the Russian government requested from the All-Union authorities permission to use the second national channel, the response was negative. The republic was allowed to use only four hours of television time daily: two on the first channel and two on the second. This inevitably increased tensions between the two governments and the two presidents.

There was a nationwide scandal when a broadcast of Yeltsin's interview, taped for the All-Union TV, was postponed. It was no wonder that the republics and their leaders were highly sensitive about their newly acquired independence. This was even more true of Yeltsin, who came to power with the bitter opposition of the Communist party apparat and Gorbachev personally. The latter used every possible means to stop his former supporter, who became his greatest rival.

The Russian Parliament took the postponement of Yeltsin's interview as an insult to the president and to the legislative body as a whole. Blame was laid on the political leaders of the country. The Parliament summoned Gosteleradio Chairman Michail Nenashev for an official explanation. Nenashev appeared even though it was Saturday. He insisted that he received no orders from Gorbachev in regard to the interview, the broadcast was postponed because of changes in schedule, and it was a personal decision. Nobody was able to prove that he was wrong. Saturday night, the interview was aired but the tension between the Union and republican officials persisted. This left unanswered the question of actual or potential misuse of its monopoly power by Gosteleradio.

In December 1990 Radio Rossiya went on air. The station, a division of the All-Russian Radio and Television company (VRTK), was provisionally using Gosteleradio frequencies. But it was administratively independent of the central authority and financed by the RSFSR. It broadcast several hours daily on three different channels.

The Russian administration supported and patronized the journalists whom the All-Union authorities were trying to oust. Yeltsin offered the team of the "Vzglyad" program and to the Interfax news agency a means of retreat. "Vzglyad" was cancelled late in December 1990 then taken under the auspices of RSFSR State Radio and Television and scheduled to start operation in March 1991. Three of its moderators—Alexandr Politkovsky, Alexandr Lyubimov, and Vladimir Mukusev—were members of the RSFSR Congress of People's Deputies.

After its resumption as a pro-Yeltsin and anti-Gorbachev program, "Vzglyad" lasted for several more months. By the end of 1991 it passed the peak of its popularity. The concept of the program was based entirely on criticism of the Communist party and the All-Union authorities, which by this time were eliminated. Actually, the very object of the program has disappeared, the goal it pursued was achieved, and it is no wonder that the program itself has quietly gone. Its team continues to work under a name "VID" (Russian abbreviation for "Vzglyad and the others") producing other programs.

The Soviet authorities closed the Interfax offices and seized its equipment in a financial dispute. But Yeltsin's administration quickly provided new premises belonging to the Russian Federation and the agency resumed operation.

The republics had a well founded mistrust of the major All-Union media. Their information was often selective and distorted, especially on the most sensitive issues such as ethnic conflicts or relationships between the Center and the powers at lower levels. Commenting on Yeltsin's interview, *Moscow news* stated, "We seem to have not learned from our recent experience with the Baltic Republics, when Moscow mass media played a fatal role by providing no timely opportunities for the sides to have a calm and detailed dialogue, and thereby allowed the events to take a course which was far from the best."[19]

We should add that if Russia had a television channel of its own, this kind of conflict with the central authorities might not have occurred.

THE LIMITS OF FREEDOM: THE CASE
OF LENINGRAD TV

The fight for television occurred at every level of power, becoming sharper when democratic forces gained obvious new victories. (The conflict around Yeltsin's postponed interview also occurred soon after he was elected the chairman of the Supreme Soviet of Russia, an event that the central authorities did their best to prevent.) The first thing the establishment structures tried to do was to affirm their authority over the news media. Some less important battles might be lost to win the most important ones. The establishment naturally provoked the resistance of other political forces. The incident that the official press labeled "an invasion to the Leningrad television station" is a perfect illustration of this.

The Leningrad channel became the best in the country in the late 1980s, but only a relatively small part of the population could watch it. Actually, only two programs, generated this good reputation: a local evening news report, "600 seconds," and a documentary, "The fifth wheel" (it was on twice a week); most of its other programs were mediocre.

Within a short period "600 seconds" became the highest rated if not the only American-style local news program on Soviet TV. It was sensational, revealing, investigative, and seemingly independent of power institutions, frequently tapping nonofficial sources of information. The brilliant reporter Alexandr Nevzorov, the star of the program, made it famous. Everyone in the area watched "600 seconds"; according to local TV ratings, 99½ percent of viewers watched.

Gosteleradio Chairman Michail Nenashev had a different opinion. He admitted that he did not like the program, because "it is based on shocking information" that is not good for the Soviet people, who "even without that are irritated today by multifold troubles."[20] "600 seconds" did not comfort the audience as the state TV head would have liked.

"Victims" of Nevzorov, people whose crimes or misdoings he exposed, did not like the broadcast either. They preferred to go without publicity. They often threatened the journalist and once he was shot and wounded by a man who had claimed that he wanted to give Nevzorov information for a story.

Unfortunately, Nevzorov did not feel like remaining a city reporter. He decided to go into politics on the side of the conservatives. A turning point of his career occurred after the events in Lithuania when he shot the documentary "Nashi" (Ours), which praised the troops that captured the TV tower in Vilnius. The reporter alleged that the fatalities were caused by heart attacks and road accidents. The Ministry of Defense awarded Nevzorov a medal for his reporting. In the documentary "Pan-opticum" Nevzorov accused Michail Gorbachev of "state betrayal." Some periodicals wrote about his connections with KGB. Thus, in 1991 a criminal reporter became one of the leading figures of the conservative movement in Russia.[21]

"The fifth wheel" was the other highly rated program on Leningrad TV. It became a unifying force for the local democratic intelligentsia. We should remember that Leningrad is not just a large city, an industrial and cultural center; it is also considered the second capital of the country. Behind this program there was also a bright personality in journalism, Bella Kurkova, who is also a political figure: she was elected a member of the Parliament of Russia.

Although the local authorities were unhappy about these programs, in the political atmosphere of perestroika they could not ignore public reaction completely and do what they liked. There were attempts to censor "The fifth wheel" and to postpone some of its episodes. Twice, when the changes in the program imposed by the authorities were too substantial, the crew itself refused to air the program and those "holes" in the regular schedule aroused public protests against censorship. Bella Kurkova received administrative reprimands for inviting undesirable guests. A number of accounting commissions were sent to control the business side of program activities. Now and then, rumors that the "Wheel" would be banned circulated. But it survived, raising the astounding question, Why? That's how unusual the situation was.

The regional party committee was hesitant about direct interference for a long time, even though that had been the usual way of dealing with problems. These dissidents were discussed at a committee meeting and its decisions were binding on every institution within the territory. When the committee finally decided to debate the problem of TV dissidents at a plenary meeting, it still vacillated about prohibiting the program; it only expressed its dissatisfaction with it. The most important decision was that television should think over its "cadre policy" and modify it.[22]

Before perestroika that would have been a disastrous verdict, meaning that dissenting journalists must be reprimanded by their Communist party organization (if they were members) and be dismissed from their jobs with an uncertain prospect for finding new jobs in the media.

But public support of "The fifth wheel" was so wide and vigorous and the movement for its defense was so strong that the 1989 decision had no effect: "To be or not to be the "Wheel' for the city was almost synonymous with the question whether democracy is real or can be suppressed by just one order."[23] Democracy won that battle, but it was not the end of the war.

When the democratic forces gained a majority in the local elections in the spring of 1990, the regional party committee adopted the resolution "About changes in the structure of the Leningrad press and the other mass media." It turned over the ownership of the major local paper, *Leningradskaya pravda*, which used to be published jointly by the party and by the city and the regional Soviets, to the party. The city Soviet was awarded an evening newspaper, *Vecherny Leningrad* (*Evening Leningrad*), and the regional Soviet received nothing.[24] There was nothing special about this resolution. A similar one was made in Moscow and the pattern was routinely repeated throughout the country.

Was it just a coincidence that the Gosteleradio chairman, Michail Nenashev, visited Leningrad at about the same time? Officially the visit was not mentioned at all, and one could only guess at its aims. But according to the press, Nenashev offered the regional TV committee new equipment, a wider zone of broadcasting, and higher salaries. All this was to be bartered for new status for the committee, which had become an affiliate of the central television.[25]

The version of the events that later appeared in the official newspaper *Izvestiya* and referred to a press conference by Nenashev was a bit different. The report did not mention the visit to Leningrad or any changes proposed there (if there were any) but indicated that Nenashev brought up the Council of Ministers resolution of 1979. The resolution stated the intention to organize an All-Union program at the Leningrad station. The official document was interpreted in such a way that Leningrad TV was already an affiliate of the Central TV.[26]

There is no reason to doubt that the document might really have existed but the question is why it surfaced at that particular moment. It was definitely a political decision, implying that if the Leningrad station was a part of the Central TV, the newly elected democratic local legislature would have no authority over it.

To be fair it must also be admitted that the structure of the Soviet television management was objectively quite complicated, especially at lower levels. It was officially responsible to several organizations and informally responsible to others that acted unofficially but were nevertheless even more influential.

The Leningrad Committee for Television and Radio Broadcasting was officially subordinate to three authorities: the Leningrad City Soviet, the Regional Soviet, and Gosteleradio. But all that was more of a formality, especially in the first two cases, since Gosteleradio provided funding and supplies. The real authority resided in the Regional Committee of the CPSU, which had the power to appoint the highest-level officers to every important institution in the region, including TV—it was called "pursueing cadre policy." The headmen of the Leningrad TV Committee were party appointees; some of them were apparatchiks before they managed broadcasting.

The conflict between the new democratic City Soviet and the TV authorities once more revealed the fight over exercising control of the news media. This time, the immediate cause of the clash was an attempt to abolish a TV program by Nikolai Ivanov, the criminal investigator and Parliament member discussed previously. But the roots of the conflict were much deeper.

Ivanov was elected a people's deputy in Leningrad, as well as a criminal investigator who probed cases of corruption in government structures. Speaking on local TV, he promised to report additional details uncovered by the investigation on his next show. A day before the presentation was scheduled, the chairman of the Leningrad committee for television and radio, Boris Petrov, a former party apparatchik, announced that it would be canceled.

The announcement provoked the strongest reaction from the City Soviet, which demanded that the TV station be subordinate to the Soviet, that Petrov be fired, and that Ivanov get his air time. Above all, a group of deputies went to the station the evening "600 seconds" was on the air and Alexandr Nevzorov gave his chair to Nikolai Ivanov. The broadcast was interrupted immediately, and after a pause filled by a documentary, an anchorwoman announced that the schedule had been revised and Ivanov would speak.[27]

This turned out to be the only result of an ugly confrontation in which both sides acted badly. Fighting illegitimacy by illegitimate methods cannot possibly be productive. This practice was habitual in the old system and natural to it. But a democratically elected legislative institution is supposed to use other means to achieve its goals.

Here's the end of the story: after the incident it was decided "for the sake of better use of transmitters" to route the Leningrad telecast through the Ostankino television center in Moscow.[28]

It was no wonder, that Leningrad TV, run jointly by Gosteleradio and local authorities, was seeking independence. It announced its intention to leave the Soviet state broadcasting system, end the series of conflicts, and become an independent company. A group of Leningrad intellectuals signed a letter demanding independence and criticizing the policy of Gosteleradio. But as it turned out it was not the only institution inclined to control Leningrad TV and radio.

The Leningrad City Soviet voted to create an independent broadcasting company. It stated that the regional TV and radio committee was trying to revive censorship. The working collective of Leningrad TV rejected this plan of the local Soviet on the grounds that it constituted interference by the legislature in the activities of the company. Of course the All-Union TV and Radio Company turned down the request, too. It kept exercising control until the Soviet Union disintegrated and the central structures collapsed.

During glasnost people came to understand that an unexpected break in a regular TV schedule meant that the announced program was vetoed because it was too controversial. They may not have been right in every case, but in the long run their suspicions were well founded, although officially those suspicions were rarely confirmed.

A two-day cancellation of Leningrad TV broadcasting to Moscow and other regions at the end of June started many rumors even though a preliminary announcement had been made. It explained that Leningrad TV had overstepped the bounds of its air time by broadcasting too many public affairs programs, including sessions of the local and the regional Soviets. In simple terms, it had overspent the funds for paying the Ministry of Communications for transmission. Both mainstream and alternative newspapers interviewed TV officials in Leningrad and Moscow, trying to find out what had really happened. They published the expense figures, which supported the official version, but those figures varied in different newspapers.[29]

Nevertheless, the mistrustful people suspected that they were being deprived of their favorite channel because some controversial programs were planned and the authorities did not want them on the air. Besides, there was no answer as to why those exact two days, June 26 and 27, 1990, were chosen to interrupt the transmission from Leningrad. Furthermore, solving television problems, however serious, at the expense of viewers did not seem to be the most appropriate method.

The history of perestroika and post-perestroika is full of paradoxes and surprises. When democratic opposition came to power it quickly forgot its democratic principles. If we take the media field, Bella Kurkova has provided an amazing example of this. In October 1992, as the most active supporter of Yeltsin, she was appointed by president's decree to head the former Leningrad TV and radio company, reorganized into Federal TV and radio broadcasting service "Rossiya." The reorganization meant that the company got a higher stature and was placed under a direct supervision of somebody trusted personally by the president.

Several months later, in March 1993, Kurkova did to her subordinate Nevzorov what Soviet authorities used to do to "Vzglyad": she banned his broadcast. His conservative, Communist, nationalist, chauvinistic opinions were pointed to as grounds for it. It is difficult to believe that this action was taken by one of the strongest media supporters of glasnost and perestroika. Democrats won press freedom but as it turns out, they mean it only for those who share their views, not for the opposition. It looks like the establishment of anti-Communist censorship instead of Communist. The rulers are inclined to abuse their power whenever they can, irrespective of their ideology. This is a worrisome lesson taught by prohibition of Nevzorov's program.

Another lesson, much more optimistic, is that as a result of the years of glasnost the authorities cannot ignore public opinion, however they try. Nevzorov's supporters started near the TV center around-the-clock meeting demanding to lift the ban. The meeting lasted for over a week, and as a result the program was resumed.

Arbitrary rules that limit press freedom for whatever reason are very dangerous. Either freedom of the press exists for everyone, or it does not exist at all.

"PUT ME ON TRIAL," A JOURNALIST ASKS

Television viewers were not the only ones suffering from power abuses by the monopoly structure of state television. Journalists' experiences were even more painful. The relationships of the most outspoken with the authorities were always uneasy and they still are. They were not only allowed to say more during glasnost than before but could also discuss their problems in the press, appealing to public opinion for support. They strove for freedom of the press but Gosteleradio officials still thought that many problems in television resulted from the inefficiency of "the system of management and organization of a creative process,"[30] however ridiculous this may sound.

The history of Soviet television in the late 1980s and early 1990s reflected the political struggle in the society. It illustrated the victories of the left-wing forces and the deeply rooted immutability of the Communist power structures, standing firmly against the new winds. The new structures existed paradoxically within the old system they opposed. Neither was strong enough to take over absolutely.

It was the same on television. The struggle was almost visible. There were some liberal programs but they could suddenly disappear for a while or forever. There were dissenting voices on the screen, but journalists could sometimes be punished for letting them on the air or for making comments of their own. Reporters could report on military actions against demonstrators, but the broadcasts revealing why the actions were taken and who was responsible were cut off.

As a matter of fact, a large stratum of the party and the government bureaucracy in the Soviet Union blamed the mass media for many of society's problems. They were masters of this country and they were used to a friendly information environment. Silencing of undesirable, disturbing information created the false but comfortable impression that everything was for the best in this best of worlds.

When numerous troubles and pains of the society under glasnost, flooded newspaper pages and TV screens the conservative sector of the establishment reacted as if real life wasn't ugly; only the media's depiction of it was. They would have liked to revive the custom of killing the messenger who bore bad news, but since that was impossible, they demanded that the media be prevented from speaking freely. When no bad news is reported, it appears that nothing has happened.

The All-Russian Party Conference in the summer of 1990 was a founding congress of the Communist party of Russia. This conference and the 28th Congress of the CPSU were dominated by conservative apparatchiks. Both meetings condemned the media for misbehavior as one of their dominant themes. The same thing happened at the plenary meetings of the Central Committee of the CPSU and at party conferences at different levels.

At its first session, the 28th Congress discussed how the media should cover the event and decided to arrange a commission "on relations with the press."[31] While the question was being discussed, one of the delegates made a meaningful slip of the tongue when, in accordance with usual party practice, he offered to create a group "to control" the media coverage. The formula was rejected but the approach to the problem remained the same. The congress also decided that the sessions should not be broadcast in full.

Within a few days, the Congress discussed the mass media again because many people in the audience were not satisfied with the media coverage of the event, especially television's. Some delegates heatedly protested. The speakers complained that "some correspondents express their opinions" when commenting on the sessions of the Congress and the most determined delegates demanded that "the members of the Commission on relations with the press must be fighters and expose the press when it is lying."[32] Intolerance prevailed at the highest Communist party gathering and all the dissenting opinions were denounced and absolutely rejected.

Still, some delegates recognized that the decision not to broadcast the entire meeting was a mistake. They had forgotten again that the TV and radio system was not officially subordinate to the party. The Congress reversed its own decision and demanded that Gosteleradio broadcast the sessions in full, though not live. Gosteleradio obeyed the party's orders again; there is no question about that.

In spite of numerous declarations about the separation of the party from the state, pronounced at the highest level of government in the Soviet Union, the practice was quite different. The TV system was as subordinate to the party as it had always been in spite of its formal stature. The Constitution no longer declared the leading role of the Communist party in the society (it had not done so in Stalin's time, by the way), but this role and the real hegemony of the party still existed. Whatever Nenashev said about Soviet television's belonging to the "state," it was first and foremost a party controlled and managed system.

Nevertheless, the nomenklatura felt its power threatened and tried to fight back. One of the principal speakers at the Congress of the Communist party of Russia, I. Osadchy, used military terms to describe the CPSU as "armlessly sitting in trenches under a heavy fire of quickly organized anti-socialist forces. Some mass media," he said, "have played an important role in their consolidation, alongside with rather contradictory, sometimes unpredictable policy of the party leadership." A newspaper recorded that the speaker was rewarded with "a burst of applause."[33]

The old forces criticized the media because the messenger who carried bad news was always guilty. The media were also the most influential instruments of democratic change, at least the most visible of them. The nomeklatura perceived the mass media in general, with the exception of the most conservative elements, as a hostile institution. Speaking at the RSFSR Writers' Union Congress, the chairman of its board, Yuri Bondarev, reportedly maintained that "under perestroika the media have done more harm than the Nazi invasion."[34]

It is noteworthy that the deeper the changes were, the stronger the opposition of the conservative establishment was. Journalists felt that the pressures on them were not becoming lighter but heavier as glasnost continued. The decreasing number of live broadcasts was an obvious sign of the pressure.

One Soviet TV commentator Igor Fesunenko, stated that the pressure he and his colleagues experienced was coming from outside the system: "The Chairman of the Committee, and after him all of us feel some strong pressure from the top, and it is the stronger, the higher the tension in the country is." He stressed that both the middle-level party functionaries and secretaries of the republican Communist parties assumed that the journalists were guilty of everything. "The pressure was growing, and our management was forced to step back and, in its turn, was pressing on broadcast journalists."[35]

His colleague, Vladimir Tsvetov, referred to a complaint against him signed by fifty secretaries of lower-level party organizations at one of the Moscow enterprises. They criticized the so-called monopoly of anchormen. This expression had become a commonplace among right-wing critics of TV although there are a dozen anchormen.[36]

Until the very end of the Soviet Union, it was not Gosteleradio itself or even the Council of Ministers that made the decisions that affected television. The Central Committee of the Communist party actually made these decisions in the most important cases, the Politburo. The "7 days" Sunday night program was cancelled on its "recommendation" (the party has never ordered anything, it just advises or recommends). The authorities were actually unhappy about the program's liberal moderator, Alexandr Tichomirov, and wanted to remove him from the air.

The official explanation, however, cited "viewers' letters" demanding the return of the program that was previously shown in that time slot. This reference to "people's requirement" and "people's support" was widely used in the mass propaganda to justify official policies. Many crimes have been committed in Soviet history under this banner, from the mass persecutions of the 1930s to the dissidents' imprisonments and expulsions of the 1970s.

The party leaders got what they wanted but they experienced a boomerang effect as they had in a number of other situations: Tichomirov was elected a people's deputy of the Russian republic and so were his younger colleagues, the moderators of a highly popular program, "Vzglyad." "Vzglyad" had been criticized many times by officials, often censored, scandalously suspended, and entirely banned at last. "Almost every 'Vzglyad,' wrote one moderator, Dmitry Zakharov, "came on air as if a T-34 tank after a duel against a dozen cannons—all damaged and smashed."[37]

Those in charge of TV everywhere can control program content and do so now and then. But in a competitive environment censorship is much less of a problem than in a monopolistic structure. The actual lawlessness of the Soviet TV system and absence of any regulation encouraged the so-called telephone rule (discussed later) here. In this respect, TV was no different from other spheres of life in the Soviet Union.

The bureaucracy adapted itself to the era of glasnost and changed some of its methods. Before perestrioka, if the management did not like a program, a comment, or a point of view expressed by a journalist, he or she was officially reprimanded in a written order that was placed on a billboard for everyone's information. There are no direct orders now, journalists complain; you are just quietly moved off the air or ordered to cover cultural life instead of politics. This is usually done by a telephone call "from the top," and a call, as they say in Russia, cannot be put into a file. There is no proof of its existence; nevertheless it is quite effective.

In protesting these methods a young TV journalist, Vladimir Flyarkovsky, asked to be given an open, honest trial to determine his, guilt. He preferred this way of deciding his and his colleagues' professional fate to the way it had been done—"there are no tracks, just one telephone call."[38]

THE PRESIDENT'S DECREES: DID THEY SOLVE THE PROBLEMS?

The decree "On democratization and development of television and radio broadcasting in the USSR"[39] signed by Michail Gorbachev on summer 1990 was the first significant act of the state in this field under perestroika.

The timing of this decree clearly demonstrated that the reason for its appearance was the intention of the new Russian leadership, headed by Gorbachev's political rival Yeltsin, to obtain one of the Soviet national channels for republican broadcasting. The decree proclaimed the illegitimacy of all acts of the republican and lower bodies "intended to change legal and proprietorship stature of the working units of the State Committee of the USSR for Television and Radio Broadcasting." It was an anti-Russian declaration since all the other republics already ran their own broadcasting, regardless of whether they declared it independent of Gosteleradio or were still subordinate to it.

Ignoring the real practice, the president (and the head of the Communist party) declared that "monopolizing of air time by one or another party, political movement, or group is impermissible, as is rerouting the state television and radio broadcasting to the means of propaganda of the personal political view of its staff members." The last remark was a reflection of the conservative criticism of "the monopoly of anchormen," or, in other words, the publicizing of facts that the authorities didn't want scrutinized.

The decree claimed, "The functions of the state television must be fulfilled independently of political and social organizations, to serve objective and all-sided coverage of the processes, going on in the country." But how could Gosteleradio be independent of political organizations if its chairman was a member of the Communist party and in fact its Central Committee?

On the positive side, the document stated the need "to determine a legal basis" for broadcasting activities in the new situation; it recommended that the Supreme Soviet adopt a specific law. The decree also stated that the Soviets of People's Deputies at all levels, public organizations, and parties had the right to open new TV centers or studios at their own expense or to rent air time from Gosteleradio. The document ordered the start of a licensing system. Gosteleradio was told to develop one with the Ministry of Justice. The question is whether an executive body should have the right to draft a law that is supposed to regulate, among other things, its own activities. Of course, this was a tradition of the Soviet system, but it did not have to be preserved.

This seemed to open new possibilities for the other players in the game except Gosteleradio but still only in theory. In practice, matters were gloomier. First, there was no market in broadcasting equipment. The supply of existing production facilities did not even cover the demand of the studios that were on the air at the time the decree was issued. No one expected that the equipment would be sold on a free market. Besides, its technical quality was lower than that of foreign equipment. But that was not the greatest problem.

The most difficult problem for a commercial station, wrote the newspaper *Commersant*, a publication for and about newly emerging Soviet businesses, was obtaining a frequency. According to the existing procedures, only ministries or other state bodies (owners of radio stations) could apply for a frequency from the State Inspectorate of Electrocommunications, a department of the Ministry of Communications. This procedure does not allow for the creation of independent TV and radio stations that did not belong to state institutions.[40]

In fact, all broadcasting frequencies are controlled by the Ministry of Communications and are generally used by Gosteleradio and the military. Until then, the only way for a commercial station to obtain a frequency was to arrange a joint venture with either the Ministry of Communications or Gosteleradio.

A new system of licensing was drafted by Gosteleradio but it was not approved officially. It was a complicated three-stage system. The first step was obtaining a registration certificate. The application must state the kind of broadcasting, the form of transmission, and the sources of finance. The second stage was obtaining a broadcast frequency. Only those who had financial means and broadcasting equipment were eligible. The third, and supposedly the longest stage, was getting permission to broadcast.

One wonders whether this system was really designed to encourage the development of alternative stations or to hinder it. The draft regulation on licensing proves that the critics of the presidential decree were right when they read between the lines and saw a desire "not to let power go out of collapsing structures."[41]

The second and the least important decree in this sphere issued by Michail Gorbachev was called "On creation of an All-Union State Television and Radio Broadcasting Company," published in February 1991.

The decree appeared to be only a change of signs because the new organization inherited all the property, assets, and functions of Gosteleradio. The decree also established an All-Union Council "to improve coordination of research and development and program policy" of the republics under the chairmanship of the head of the company. It would not have been clear why the decree was issued except for one point: The president appointed Leonid Kravchenko chairman of the company.

Kravchenko had been nominated to head Gosteleradio late in November 1990 but, according to the law, the appointment needed to be approved by the Supreme Soviet of the USSR. His first actions as acting chairman of Gosteleradio, including the ban of "Vzglyad," were widely criticized by the public and by liberal politicians. That could have complicated his confirmation. But as a head of a state company he could be appointed directly by the president. Thus, Gorbachev guaranteed that his protégé would run TV and radio in spite of any criticism by the public or legislators.

Leonid Kravchenko himself provided the most detailed comment on the short text of the decree. At his first press conference as the head of the new institution that replaced Gosteleradio on February 11, 1991, he confirmed that the change would make him a subordinate to President Gorbachev alone. In its report on the conference, TASS omitted this comment. At the press conference Kravchenko again rejected the idea of sharing Gosteleradio's TV and radio equipment with the newly created broadcasting company of the Russian Federation.

He stated that the formation of the All-Union Television and Radio Company would broaden the rights of republican broadcasting organizations. He said that from then on the republican committees on TV and radio would be free. The central authorities would hardly agree to this, but for the republics' declarations of sovereignty. They were supposed to cooperate in the All-Union Council, headed by Kravchenko, too, according to the decree. But he promised that all its members would have equal rights.

Kravchenko said the same to the heads of the republican broadcasting companies when he met with them to discuss the prospects of the new council. They were supposed to cooperate within this structure. The head of RSFSR TV and radio broadcasting, Anatoly Lysenko, said that the council would be a positive innovation only if all its members were equal, as Kravchenko promised at his press conference. Since then, however, Kravchenko had continued to interfere arbitrarily in the work of the republican companies. That meant that half-measures in the president's decree weren't working. They simply could not work because they were in conflict with the old power structure, which was still more or less in the same position.

ENOUGH POLITICS: LONG LIVE ENTERTAINMENT!

The cadre shifts at the highest level of management of Soviet media late in 1990 seemed puzzling at the beginning. Gorbachev changed pieces as on the board if he were playing political chess: Michail Nenashev was moved back to Goskompechat, which he had previously left to manage Gosteleradio, and Leonid Kravchenko was returned from TASS to the chairmanship of the Gosteleradio, where he had worked earlier. Those shifts were very important as a reflection of a move to the right in Gorbachev's politics. But they were also meaningful in their influence on the politics of the national media, television in particular. There could hardly have been any optimistism about the implications of those cadre shifts late in 1990; if anyone still had some illusions, they were soon, dispelled.

After Kravchenko took over Gosteleradio, criticism of Gorbachev on television was censored as it had been under his predecessor.[42] As under Nenashev, the "Vzglyad" program on New Year's Eve was banned. It was about Foreign Minister Shevardnadze, who had just dramatically resigned after warning of a coming dictatorship in the Soviet Union.[43] Kravchenko denied that he had banned the show but admitted that he had "advised" that an interview with Shevardnadze would not be "appropriate."[44] The audience of this weekly show was estimated at 90 million.

The moderators of "Vzglyad" said that they were originally promised by Kravchenko that the program would be shown in a week but that he informed them later that the program would be banned entirely.[45]

One of the journalists on the show, Alexandr Politkovsky, told Radio Liberty's Russian Service that Pyotr Reshetov, the first deputy chairman of Gosteleradio, had signed an order suspending the production and broadcast of "Vzglyad" for an indefinite time.[46]

The new Gosteleradio chairman actually supported Nenashev's idea of "comforting" people. He declared that Soviet TV would avoid "excessive politicization." There would be "a sharp increase in non-factual programming, with more films and plays, musical and entertainment programs, and television quizzes" that would help people "to lose themselves."[47] His ideal for television was like Nenashev's: TV was not political; it was "preachery, spiritual, artistic."[48] The suspension of "Vzglyad," which had too much (and too liberal) politics, corresponded fully to that ideal.

"The thaw is over" was the comment of the oldest anchorman of Soviet television, Igor Kirillov.[49] In the political lexicon of the Soviet Union, "thaw" used to refer to a short period in the history of the country—the time of liberalization under Khrushchev. It appeared to many people that the question of whether perestroika meant the end of the winter or just a thaw had received a discouraging answer.

This pessimism was supported by the fact that "Vzglyad" was not the only victim; several other programs were also scheduled for cancellation. Kravchenko had developed the concept of his predecessor further by removing not only "Vzglyad" but other liberal documentaries. In Moscow democrats staged a demonstration to protect glasnost. Several thousand people gathered in the center of the city to support "Vzglyad."

Not only was glasnost violated and the viewer choice limited as a result of the authorities' actions; dozens of employees of the central TV were affected as well. An independent news agency, Interfax, an alternative to TASS, was a joint venture sponsored by Gosteleradio that operated on its premises; it was also closed indefinitely. Luckily the government of the Russian republic permitted it to continue to operate.

By his first actions as head of Gosteleradio, Leonid Kravchenko made it quite obvious why Gorbachev had chosen him in a shift to the right. Kravchenko had strongly confirmed his reputation as the most conservative figure in the highest echelon of Soviet media management. In view of later developments in Soviet politics it became clear that Kravchenko's appointment was just another signal of a reverse in Gorbachev's domestic policies, which he made under pressure from hardliners.

People in charge of the system might change but as long as the system survived, it kept working as it had been programmed to. And as time passed, fewer hopes remained that it could be radically restructured from the top. As a result, until the very collapse of the Union, there was a high degree of uncertainty about how the future of the broadcasting system in the Soviet Union was going to look.

And it was not just a matter of underdeveloped legislative foundations. Under perestroika, it also became evident that however important the central authorities were, they could not be the only active players in this game any longer. It would be impossible to impose rules they felt comfortable with on the others—the republican and local authorities, the new political parties, and the new businesses—especially if their interests were ignored. If the new rules of the game were designed to preserve the advantages of one side (as the presidential decrees and existing projects for restructuring had been), it seemed highly doubtful that the other players would obey them in that time of turmoil.

CRACKDOWN IN LITHUANIA: THE SYSTEM FIGHTS BACK

Of course there were always tanks, the ultimate argument of any dictatorship, available. And the tragic experience of Bloody Sunday, January 13, in Vilnius dispelled the illusion that this argument would not be used. It is symbolic that people died defending the television tower that provided independent broadcasting and free expression in the republic. Defense Minister Yazov defended this brutal action by saying it was necessary to stop anti-Soviet propaganda. He revealed that imperial thinking still prevailed among the central authorities and they were ready to impose their ideas by all means including military force. Nor was there any guarantee that force would not be used in other regions.

President Gorbachev and the other top Soviet officials denied that they sanctioned the military operation or even knew about it. But a group of independent investigators said that the Kremlin planned a crackdown in Lithuania. Three days before the attack, a functional space telecommunications center, directly connected to Moscow, was installed at a military base in Vilnius. According to investigators, this fact indicated that the Kremlin had immediate access to information from Vilnius. The authors concluded that the action on January 13, 1991, was planned, approved, and coordinated by the central leadership, including President Gorbachev, well in advance.[50]

A dis-information campaign in the mainstream Soviet media was conducted. After the crackdown in Lithuania, an official with censorship functions was appointed to Television Service of News (TSN) and to "Vremya." But the first signs of the new wave of authoritarian control over the news media were felt earlier.[51]

TSN was soon banned because its coverage of the events in the Baltics was notably more objective than that of "Vremya." On January 15, it showed the corpses of people shot during the violence on Sunday and the tanks in the streets of Vilnius.

Soviet Defense Minister Dmitri Yazov accused certain newspapers of slander on the "Vremya" evening news program: *Nezavisimaya gazeta*, *Moskovsky komsomolets*, and *Komsomolskaya pravda*.

The highest military officers used their authority to organize assistance for Leonid Kravchenko. Army units were ordered to conduct a telegram campaign in support of the conservative head of the All-Union Gosteleradio. The directive praised Kravchenko's policies in regard to the military forces.[52]

A famous Leningrad reporter, Alexandr Nevzorov, had sided with the army on Lithuania. His broadcast "Nashi" (Ours) justified the crackdown. It was shown by Leningrad TV and twice in prime time by both channels of the national television.

But it ignored a ruling of the Supreme Soviet of the USSR that approved a resolution urging national TV to present the point of view of the other side. The legislators offered to screen films available in the Lithuanian consulate in Moscow that gave the Baltic point of view.

In a call-in TV program Leonid Kravchenko and his deputy Pyotr Reshetov defended the policies of Gosteleradio. In responding to hostile calls, they said that their critics understood the word *truth* differently. The officials insisted that it was not the Union authorities but the Baltic parliaments who were to blame for the military crackdown in their republics. They said, that this was the message Central TV tried to give its viewers.[53]

But we are not living in 1940. The government has lost its total control over the mass media and large-scale misinformation campaigns are not as effective as they used to be. Even violent military actions like the one in Lithuania were meaningless; the battle was lost the moment it started. Tanks could prolong the agony of the empire but not save it. The world is different from what it was fifty or even twenty years ago. The climate has created optimism and hope that glasnost will ultimately become real freedom of the press. The taste of freedom is unforgettable.

After the military takeover of the Vilnius TV tower, an alternative TV station began broadcasting just five days later from the building that housed the Lithuanian parliament. The Kaunas TV station that was on the air only two and a half hours a week began to broadcast all day.

Vilnius TV resumed programming with army colonel Edmundas Kasperavicius, dressed in civilian clothing, as the main anchorman. Many people who worked at Vilnius TV refused to resume their jobs until the army withdrew. Fifteen hundred workers at Vilnius TV and radio, whose offices were seized January 13, demanded that their facilities be returned to them. They decided that rotating groups would go on hunger strikes for one or two days until the military evacuated the facilities.

In Moscow, about sixty leading Soviet cultural figures decided to boycott the Soviet Central TV until the censorship imposed on it by Gosteleradio Chairman Leonid Kravchenko was lifted. They signed an open letter saying that political censorship had been revived and, as a result, TV viewers were receiving an incomplete and distorted picture of events. In the letter published by *Komsomolskaya pravda* on January 24, celebrities stated that they would not appear on TV until RSFSR republican broadcasting began. Some other cultural personalities joined the boycott later in a protest against the distorted coverage of the events in Lithuania and Latvia.

Altogether, over two hundred leading cultural figures supported the boycott. The Moscow organization of cinema workers joined protests against censorship and misinformation on Soviet TV. The filmmakers elaborated that the boycott would apply only to entertainment shows on Central TV, not to Moscow and Leningrad local TV and not to certain liberal political programs. Since some full-time employees of Central TV had opted to join the boycott, the filmmakers voted to set up a special "Foundation in the defense of glasnost" to help them survive.

The politics of the TV authorities were also condemned at the session of the Supreme Soviet of Russia. In February 1991, the Supreme Soviet also approved a draft law amending the RSFSR criminal code, which makes obstructing the professional activities of journalists a criminal offense. Officials who used their position to hinder the work of journalists could be removed from their jobs by the court. Leonid Kravchenko was considered a possible target of the new law.[54]

The Moscow branch of the Union of Journalists of the USSR accused Kravchenko of reimposing censorship on Soviet television and excluded him from membership in the Union.

TV REFORMS: RUNNING IN PLACE

During the last years of perestroika, state television experienced more cadre changes on the highest level than ever before. These appointments were important because they indicated shifts to liberalism or to a hard line in the politics of the president. But they could never have solved the major problem of Soviet television: it had to be demonopolized. And the authorities never had this goal. On the contrary, control over the media was trusted to the most reliable people to protect the interests of the powers that be.

Regardless of all the shifts in politics, the "socialist choice" was the principal aim of Secretary General Gorbachev up to the collapse of the Communist party after the August 1991 putsch. Speaking at the Byelorussian Academy of Sciences in February 1991 (the speech was broadcast by Soviet TV) Gorbachev attacked the democrats and accused them of attempting to seize power by force. He denounced the "neo-Bolshevik tactics" of the radical opposition and charged that democratic groups and leaders were being directed by "alien research centers." Gorbachev said that the Soviet "left" is in reality "rightist opposition" because it rejects socialism and favors capitalism. This was probably his harshest attack on the democratic cause since the beginning of perestroika.[55]

Michail Gorbachev meant to reform the system, making it more human and efficient. And the mass media segment of the system—ideology and propaganda, as it used to be called—was treated the same way, although some dogma had to be rejected.

Obviously no change that was initiated inside the All-Union TV and Radio Company could alter its character. Introducing new organizational forms, new anchors, and new program formats did not change the structure. Has there ever been a monopoly that wanted to create a competitor for itself? The fact that the company was directly dependent on the country's leader has always offered the potential for abuse of power.

This power was surely used, sometimes in direct violation of the law. In the weeks before the March 17, 1991, referendum to decide whether the Union should stay together, radio and TV devoted considerable amounts of air time to persuading voters to say yes to the Union. They provided podiums for national patriots to convince people to vote yes. On the Friday and Saturday before the referendum, television programs were interrupted every two hours with an instructional clip, demonstrating how to cast a yes vote. On March 17, in violation of the USSR law on referendum (which forbade campaigning of any sort on the day of the vote), both radio and TV continued to urge the electorate to vote yes. In the evening, "Vremya" carried interviews with a number of people who characterized the attempt to agitate against the referendum as "violation of human rights."[56]

Only an alternative TV structure could provide a counterbalance in this situation and others and democratize the television of this country.

Yeltsin used the TV of the Russian republic as a political weapon in his struggle against Gorbachev and the central authorities. Although separate from national TV, it had inevitably inherited its characteristic features. It's another state TV except that a different leader controls it.

The official spokesman for Russian television, which started broadcasting in May 1991 admitted, "Our television can not be an alternative to the Central Television: such an alternative can come only from an independent television while we belong to the RSFSR in the same way that the Central Television belongs to the Union." The representative of Rossiiskoye televidenie made this statement at the inauguration ceremony on May 12.[57]

Russian TV was allocated six hours of broadcasting time daily on the second national channel. It started by airing an exclusive interview with Boris Yeltsin, who said that he had won the channel for the Russian Federation only after "four forceful conversations" with Gorbachev. The programming on the first days was livelier than that on Central TV. Many of the journalists had familiar faces; they had been ousted from the All-Union Company by Kravchenko.[58]

After the disintegration of the Soviet Union, Russia inherited both national channels. All the other republics except Russia had been broadcasting long before, but they were subordinate to the Center. Once the Union collapsed, they were absolutely free of any outside control but that is probably the only difference. They are state companies like Russian television. They experience strong pressure from their government and have even more problems than they used to have.

According to recent surveys in most of the Commonwealth states, if TV viewers had to choose just one channel, they would prefer Ostankino TV (the first channel of the Central TV) to republican TV. Armenia is the exception. But a substantial number of viewers considered Ostankino's coverage of events in their republic subjective.[59]

The large number of Russian speakers throughout the former Soviet Union is one obvious reason for the popularity of Ostankino. But the previous system of TV broadcasting is probably even more important. In this system, only Central TV had technical, financial, and cadre resources for gathering and distributing all the national and foreign information. Republican studios played a supplementary role: their activities were limited by the borders of the republics. They gained independence from Gosteleradio but they couldn't give their viewers enough original information about the Commonwealth states or foreign countries to compete successfully.

In this situation, it seemed natural for the Commonwealth to preserve Ostankino as a common channel. Nevertheless, the political and economic realities have been working against it. In December 1991, after the collapse of the USSR, Russia took over the All-Union TV and Radio Company. But President Yeltsin and the leaders of the other states when the Commonwealth was formed expressed their intention to use the first channel.

The plan seemed questionable from the very beginning because of the numerous differences and conflicts among the states—political, military, economic, and ethnic. It did turn out to be unworkable until at least the winter of 1993. All the other problems between the states intensified, increasing the pessimism about the future of the Commonwealth itself not just the common TV channel.

It is now Russian, funded and controlled by Moscow and perceived as such by the other Commonwealth countries. They suspect Russia of having imperialistic intentions and accuse it of planning to play the role of a new "Center." They cannot ignore this mighty country and in many respects depend on it. But they do not trust Russia and take measures to preserve their newly acquired independence. A Moscow channel is now a foreign channel to them.

The Ukraine redistributed Central TV's frequencies for its own broadcasting. The Byelorussian leader, Stanislav Shushkevich, said that he wasn't yet sure which was better for the republic: to broadcast CNN with captions or "Ostankino." He called programming from Moscow tendentious. "To my mind, 'Ostankino' will die as it lived," he claimed.[60]

Close neighbors of the Byelorussians have already had a very fruitful experience in cooperating with CNN. In spring 1991, the company gave Lithuania permission to receive its broadcasts free of charge until the end of the year. It is shown half an hour Monday through Saturday and three hours on Sunday. In return Lithuania would send information to CNN and assist its correspondents when they were working the country. CNN made similar agreements with Estonia and Latvia.

The idea of an "international" TV channel appears hopelessly idealistic not only because of differences within the Commonwealth but also because it absolutely goes against the realities of the world television market. There are a number of global TV channels now, but they are global only in distribution, not in control. Sharing of control by a number of owners in different countries (if this awkward idea has ever occurred to anybody) would cause endless disagreements and absolutely paralyze business.

Since the relations among the CIS members are quite tense, this model would be even less workable.

Ostankino is now trying to use the inertia of its past domination of the TV market of the former USSR to make it a local success and to preserve its monopoly. Opening this market to global TV exchanges would be much more fruitful. Ostankino could compete in this market, but the low quality of its programming would doom it to failure in the competition. Exchanges of television programs among the Commonwealth countries could be the first step to breaking the dominance of Ostankino (the former All-Union TV and Radio Company, former Gosteleradio) and establishing equal partnerships of the national TV companies.

Nevertheless, the management of Ostankino is working hard to make it an "international" company. Its chairman, Yegor Yakovlev, in a letter to the Commonwealth countries leaders, offered this concept of the channel and convinced them to support it.[61] The response was not enthusiastic.

Primarily Ostankino needs money, but budgets are lean everywhere in the Commonwealth. Just to pay for transmission of its programs the company needs 6 billion rubles. Of this amount 73 percent pays Russia for the transmissions. The others are supposed to pay for themselves, too, but their leaders are still undecided. The fact that they do not say yes is probably itself an answer, which Ostankino pretends not to understand.

The idea of a "channel of international communications" was conceived by the Communist party apparat long before the collapse of the Union. A resolution of the December 1990 Plenum of the Central Committee of the CPSU called for the creation of a special TV channel "Sodruzhestvo" (Russian word for *Commonwealth*). But the idea of a channel with the same name was planned by Gosteleradio as far back as the summer of 1990.

If Yakovlev's plea does not get a positive response, the two Russian TV companies may merge to make their financial burdens lighter. Two companies are better than one, no doubt. But if they are under the control of the same government, there will be little additional political diversity for the audience. Both channels are now controlled by the Yeltsin government and support it strongly.

But professional and political differences do exist between the two channels. Among the best known journalists on Russian TV (Channel 2) are those dismissed by Kravchenko from Central TV and it was originally seen as an opposition company, supporting Yeltsin against Gorbachev. But after Gorbachev resigned it lost its opposition spirit and became a loyal, conformist government channel. Ostankino (Channel 1) has always been an arm of the establishment. The appointment of Yegor Yakovlev to head it after the August putsch did not make much difference. Most of the same journalists are in its studios and much of the same conservative nomenklatura in its management.

In seeking the stature of an international company for Ostankino, its officials really seem to be fighting principally for their own future. They are powerful enough to make some Russian TV journalists worry that they would survive a merger and continue to prevail.[62] This problem would not be so painful if there were at least one alternative to state TV in the Russian republic.

The long discussed question of whether Ostankino will become an international channel has got quite an unexpected answer. In January 1993 heads of 8 Commonwealth countries—Armenia, Byelorussia, Kazakhstan, Kirgizia, Moldova, Russia, Uzbekistan, Tadjikistan—agreed to form International TV and radio company. But the most enthusiastic supporter of the idea, Yegor Yakovlev, has already been fired, and it turned out that the company does not have a channel of its own! Evidently, the Russian government, which has been in charge of the most influential channel for over a year, by this time decided not to share control over it. Until the international company gets frequencies and broadcasting facilities of its own Ostankino and Russian radio will generously provide it with 3 hours daily of TV and radio time.

TV is still caught in the vicious circle of the Communist symbiosis of the state and the media. The state is dominant, the press is instrumental, and the audience is manipulated. One can assume that it was not difficult for the journalists of Channel 1 who used to speak against Yeltsin to start defending him: they work for the state and say what they are paid to say. Without effective competition, this is the way of life. Leaders change but the state remains, and journalists speak on its behalf. They do not depend on the audience; they depend only on the officials. The Soviet authoritarian tradition is still alive.

NOTES

1. *Pravda*, February 5, 1990.
2. Ibid.
3. *Komsomolskaya pravda*, August 1, 1990.
4. Ibid.
5. Ibid.
6. *Pravda*, August 8, 1990.
7. *Moskovsky komsomolets*, January 14, 1990.
8. *Komsomolskaya pravda*, August 1, 1990.
9. Ibid.
10. Ibid.
11. Ibid.
12. *Komsomolskaya pravda*, April 19, 1990.

13. *Rabochaya tribuna*, July 7, 1990.
14. *Radio Free Europe/Radio Liberty Daily Report*, December 20, 1990.
15. *Moscow news*, 1990, No. 38.
16. Ibid.
17. *Komsomolskaya pravda*, February 10, 1990.
18. *Izvestiya*, June 28, 1990
19. *Moscow news*, 1990, N 24.
20. *Komsomolskaya pravda*, August 1, 1990.
21. *Moscow news*, No. 7, 1991; No. 26, 1991; *Nezavisimaya gazeta*, July 27, 1991.
22. *Literaturnaya gazeta*, July 18, 1990.
23. Ibid.
24. *Komsomolskaya pravda*, April 14, 1990.
25. *Literaturnaya gazeta*, April 11, 1990.
26. *Izvestiya*, April 14, 1990.
27. *Izvestiya*, April 7, 1990.
28. *Moskovsky komsomolets*, April 4, 1990.
29. *Commersant*, N 25, 1990; *Argumenty i fakty*, N 26, 1990; *Izvestiya*, June 29, 1990.
30. *Pravda*, February 5, 1990.
31. *Komsomolskaya pravda*, July 3, 1990.
32. *Izvestiya*, July 9, 1990.
33. *Sovetskaya Rossiya*, June 20, 1990.
34. *Radio Free Europe/Radio Liberty Daily Report*, December 12, 1990.
35. *Literaturnaya gazeta*, May 30, 1990.
36. Ibid.
37. *Ogonyok*, 1990, N 4, p. 25.
38. *Moscow news*, 1990, N 38.
39. *Izvestiya*, July 16, 1990.
40. *Commersant*, N 38, 1990.
41. *Demokraticheskaya Rossiya*, N 2, 1990.
42. *Radio Free Europe/Radio Liberty Daily Report*, December 20, 1990.
43. *The New York Times*, December 29, 1990.
44. *Radio Free Europe/Radio Liberty Daily Report*, January 2, 1991.
45. *Radio Free Europe/Radio Liberty Daily Report*, January 4, 1991.
46. *Radio Free Europe/Radio Liberty Daily Report*, January 11, 1991.
47. *Radio Free Europe/Radio Liberty Daily Report*, January 2, 1991.
48. *Komsomolskaya pravda*, August 1, 1990.
49. *Radio Free Europe/Radio Liberty Daily Report*, January 14, 1991.
50. *Radio Free Europe/Radio Liberty Daily Report*, March 20, 1991.
51. *Radio Free Europe/Radio Liberty Daily Report*, February 18, 1991.
52. *Radio Free Europe/Radio Liberty Daily Report*, February 20, 1991.
53. *Radio Free Europe/Radio Liberty Daily Report*, January 31, 1991.
54. *Radio Free Europe/Radio Liberty Daily Report*, March 4, 1991
55. *Financial Times*, February 28, 1991.
56. *Radio Free Europe/Radio Liberty Daily Report*, March 18, 1991.
57. *Radio Free Europe/Radio Liberty Daily Report*, May 13, 1991.
58. *Radio Free Europe/Radio Liberty Daily Report*, May 14, 1991.

59. *Izvestiya*, March 17, 1992.

60. *Nezavisimaya gazeta*, March 24, 1992.

61. Yegor Yakovlev. Kto govorit i kto pokazivaet. Pismo lideram gosudarstv chlenov SNG. *Izvestiya*, March 4, 1992.

62. Vladimir Tsvetov. Vremya i portret. *Nezavisimaya gazeta*, March 14, 1992.

4

THE IMPERATIVE OF ECONOMIC FREEDOM

FROM PROPAGANDA TO INFORMATION PRODUCTION

The evolution of the mass media under perestroika demonstrated how vital economic freedom is for them. Without it, the political and legal freedoms that have increased in this country cannot be exercised fully. Not only do readers, listeners, viewers and journalists need economic freedom; it is necessary for the society as a whole. In a country where state ownership still prevails the situation in the mass media is no exception.

The continuing dominance of state ownership in the media field encourages the abuse of power by the ruling authorities. The formation of pluralistic structures in the political and economic spheres inevitably clashed with the state-monopoly character of the largest and most influential segment of the media. This created the problem of demonopolization and creation of alternative structures.

The Soviet media were essentially a party-state monopoly that influenced all aspects of their activities:

- Financial monopoly—centralized allocation of resources from the top to the bottom
- Cadre (personnel) monopoly—centralized appointment of higher-ranking officers and editors
- Administrative monopoly—centralized distribution of paper, equipment, and other resources
- Ideological monopoly
- Political monopoly

This system served the interests not of the audience, not of the society as a whole, but of the party-government elite. With its total control over the country, it alone determined the media's well-being and prosperity. The major function of the media system has always been promotion of ideological uniformity as dictated by official doctrine.

Mass media restructuring in the country is not only a political or economic problem: it is also a problem of overcoming time-worn approaches to problems. The media have never been considered a part of the economic system, but always political and ideological tools. Money was not an issue since the media were subsidized by the state or the party. The media received funds that were sufficient for day-to-day operation but not enough to flourish.

But now the media are facing quite new realities. They must consider them in new political terms and in new and different economic terms. They will have to learn to make enough profit to support themselves and to adapt themselves to the realities of a market economy. For most of the media this is a matter of life or death.

The society needs an economic model of the media that encourages its free development. Forms of ownership other than state ownership should be established to guarantee diversity of news and views. The new media system will become an element of the emerging market economy. This will increase the effectiveness of information production and help to introduce new media technologies that other countries have been using for a long time. The result will be the satisfaction of the information consumer.

Progress has been rather poor so far. The situation resembles that in the consumer market: in neither case do people starve but they are certainly undernourished because supplies are scarce and choice is practically nonexistent particularly in audiovisual media. Thoughtful observers naturally wonder what kind of pluralistic media market will emerge in the overall reform of the Soviet economy. There can be no prosperous information market without a healthy economy, and vice versa; this is now absolutely clear.

Although the Soviet Union has fallen apart, two ways of development are still possible:

- The development of a common market for the Commonwealth of Independent States
- The breakup of the existing economic system into a number of isolated markets

The second possibility seems unproductive. It would complicate the formation of a well developed, modern media structure and would not help solve the current problems. It could make them worse. Nevertheless, a breakup seems quite possible now; very strong disintegrating trends brought about political separation. But economic interests still act as unifying forces, pulling republics toward each other and working for the preservation of the Commonwealth, at least in economic terms. That's why the first possibility seems to be more likely, though the trend to political separatism will work against it.

The common market of the new independent states, which existed as part of a large state for seventy years, actually still exists. And if it disintegrates, that will be a disaster for all the former republics of the Soviet Union. Economic crisis will deepen and market reforms will slow.

The stability and vital capacity of the Commonwealth are unclear and do not appear very promising so far. But one thing that can help it survive is the preservation of a common information market, especially in broadcasting. An agreement among the independent states about joint TV and radio broadcasting was reached only early in 1993, after a year of long negotiations. Although through all this period it was implied that Ostankino was to serve as a common channel, it turned out that it has no channel of its own. The Russian government, which has subsidized and controlled Ostankino after the collapse of the Soviet Union, decided to keep it for itself.

There are other problems and gaps between agreements and practice that are not easy to bridge. Independent states control the transmitters on their territories. They use the frequencies allocated to Moscow channels for their own broadcasts very often. Tomorrow, the very existence of a joint TV channel will mainly be a problem of loyalty to the Commonwealth.

Present political realities demand a different kind of regulation of communications between the former republics because new problems have appeared: distribution of frequencies that were centralized, transborder communications, and so on.

There is also another important reason to preserve a common audiovisual market in the former Soviet Union, a purely economic one. It will help preserve Russian as the language of interethnic communication in a huge territory with numerous ethnic groups and languages. This conglomerate wouldn't exist without a common language. The role of Russian in the Commonwealth is comparable to that of English internationally, uniting countries of the world into a global village.

All the problems of republican relations that have not yet been solved are important to the future of each republic and of the Commonwealth as a whole. Whether they do it separately or together, all the new independent states will have to develop a free economic system and a free information market.

In the United States the mass media are in tough competition for the free time of a consumer; but our situation is just the opposite: the demand for information is much higher than the supply. This is true of the rest of our economy: the producer prevails and dictates terms. And it is not only editors or TV producers who can do so: those who run printing plants and TV transmitters, the producers of newsprint and the distributers of periodicals, and so on, are also in this position. The mass media can achieve economic freedom through demonopolization of the existing state structures and diversification of forms of ownership.

The Western media have been widely criticized, and in general fairly, for their commercial character, for having profit making as their principal goal. In the Soviet Union, media scholars and journalists have raised this criticism. But now the reality of the market in the countries of the Commonwealth of Independent States requires the rejection of this hypocritical puritanism. Journalism was supposed to achieve a great ideal rather than generate petty profits. It is time to recognize that "pure" journalism in this world is an even more idealistic notion than "pure" art.

The economic realities the press faces now have suddenly made journalists and editors feel that they are in a business and this business is vulnerable. They have started to ask new questions: Who subsidizes unsuccessful publications? Who profits from the successful ones? Why can't the production of newsprint be increased when publishers are eager to pay for it? There are many questions. All of them must be answered in order to transform periodicals from tools of ideological manipulation to market entities.

Television is financed directly from the state budget. About thirty years ago it was absolutely clear who paid: TV set users were charged license fees and the fees subsidized the programming and transmission. Later direct fees were no longer charged, but indirectly they were included in the price of TV sets.

Charges of thirty to forty rubles for a TV set generated 300 million to 400 million rubles annually. Some twenty years ago that was enough to cover the budget for all TV. By 1990, this amount covered only 20 to 25 percent of Gosteleradio's budget.[1] Expenses grew primarily because of the expansion of the transmission network. The Ministry of Communications, which ran it, cost up to two thirds of the TV budget.

Since the late 1980's, Gosteleradio leaders have discussed reintroducing license fees to cover the increased costs but they have never done it. Since we have a very low standard of living, it was not difficult to foresee a mixed reaction to the plan. Nevertheless, the deteriorating economy can make the governments of Russia and the other independent states reconsider the idea. But the question is whether a license fee would be enough to cover expenses for programming and transmission over all the territory, especially in Russia which is a huge country.

The British Parliament limits the funding for the BBC to the general amount collected from the license fee. According to UNESCO statistics, there are 30 million TV sets in Britain. In this small, densely populated country, the fee generates enough money to run the BBC. In the Soviet Union (official data on separate republics have not been published so far) there are 91 million sets. A license fee would probably not produce enough revenue to cover all the expenses, especially in Russia. But even in this case, the direct funding by the audience would make TV more accountable to the public and help TV develop into a public institution, rather than a state institution.

It should not be party television as it has been for most of its history. It shouldn't be presidential as it was formally called by one of its leaders in the time of Michail Gorbachev. Nor should it be governmental, as it obviously is under the Yeltsin administration. Governments, presidents, and parties don't pay for TV; taxpayers do. And if they pay for it directly, they can demand that television serve the society and prevent the authorities from abusing public funds for their own political interests.

Introduction of this kind of public supervision would be of crucial importance because the Russian government is evidently going to keep TV under strict control in the foreseeable future. It has prohibited privatization of the existing TV system. The two national channels of the former USSR are now controlled by the Russian authorities.

Present legislation does not forbid opening of new TV companies, but the equipment for them is not sold in a free market. It is produced by state enterprises in limited quantities and distributed to existing state controlled companies. Above all, the communications infrastructure is government controlled, and it is prohibited from being privatized. In these conditions, the appearance of alternative TV channels hardly seems possible. In other words, the most pressing problem for TV—its demonopolization—cannot be solved immediately and directly. That makes the establishment of public control over TV by direct funding with license fees still more urgent.

Now and then, there are reports in the press that in some town or city district a cable system has been built. Of course, those reports indicate an important trend. For a country that just started a cable system several years ago, construction of these systems is news. But the installation of the cable is the easiest part. Having programs to broadcast on it is more difficult.

Presently, the cable channels are filled with pirated videos, movies, animated cartoons, and sometimes local advertising. But they do not have programming of their own. There are no cable networks here that could produce and distribute programming for those small systems. Thus, cable TV operates now is an entertainment medium with very limited distribution. It is not a social and political entity as in other countries, but its potential is clear. It cannot possibly compete with existing state TV now, let alone be an alternative to it.

The collapse of the USSR structures did not demonopolize anything, including TV. The difference is that now instead of one Center we have a number of centers. Each republic has its centrally controlled TV. The two Russian channels unequivocally support Boris Yeltsin's administration. Actually, there was more dissent on Central TV during perestroika than there is now.

When the production and distribution of information are monopolized by a state authority, the problem changes from an economic one into a political one. In a society that is being torn apart by numerous conflicts, there is a potential danger to the government itself. The availability of alternative information sources would help to prevent additional social tension. People who have means for expressing their views in a civilized manner and have a guarantee that those views will be considered by the society are less likely to resort to extreme actions to attract public attention to their problems.

For decades the mass media in this country lived under the pressure of Lenin's dogma that we would not make the press simply a warehouse of different views. Only one point of view could be presented. In the printed press, there is much more diversity now, but TV is still dominated by the official line. That makes the necessity for public representation even more urgent. In any case, trying to silence those who are shouting (often about pain) is a suicidal policy.

In a democratic society, the government's ideology should not dominate the mass media and public opinion as it still does here. Soviet custom is that ministries and departments make their own regulations. Thus, Gosteleradio regulated the audiovisual field and was the primary broadcaster.

Now it seems reasonable to separate those functions. TV and radio broadcasting must become more independent institutions and responsible to the public. The functions of the government here could be limited to regulating the industry. An authority like the Federal Communications Commission in the United States could do this. But it appears that the Russian government is not going to let broadcasting out of its hands.

Another factor that complicates the creation of a diversified media system is the underdevelopment of civil society. No organizations in the country (even if they were called public) were really open and voluntary in terms of membership; sometimes membership was restricted, in other cases imposed. All organizations were under total ideological supervision. Vertical structures that controlled from the top to the bottom prevailed. Nothing outside them was allowed, because that might create a potential threat to the uniformity of the society. As a result there were no organizations to promote alternative points of view.

As a civil society forms in this country, voluntary participation in numerous public and political organizations will emerge. These associations will develop a complex system of interconnections with the media system.

As the experience in other countries demonstrates, voluntary associations form a kind of a social-political infrastructure that promotes the consideration by the mass media of the interests of different societal groups. In the former Soviet Union, nothing of that kind has ever existed, and all the diversity and wealth of ties in the society were replaced by official institutions that cared only for their own interests.

Another consequence of the domination of formal structures in all spheres of life was the bureaucratic isolation of different media. They were subordinated to different departments of government. The ideology was coordinated by the Communist party but each of them worked alone to generate and distribute information.

That was another result of the dogmatic approach to the media as propaganda tools. Nobody cared about dissemination of information or about economic efficiency. A question raised by the American scholars Gladys Ganley and Oscar Ganley in the title of their book on the new information technologies *To inform or to control?*[2] was answered by the leaders of this country long ago: "to control."

There are some steps that the media themselves can take to satisfy the demand for information among the public and to raise money for their own needs. The market, even including the periodical press, is still far from satisfying all the needs of the people. In the editorial offices, only a small amount of the incoming material is actually used. It is believed that a daily newspaper actually uses only 10 percent of the information it collects. In addition, the average reader reads only 10 percent of what is published.[3]

The Media Lab of Massachusetts Institute of Technology (MIT) is already working on programs for using that lost 99 percent in a personalized electronic newspaper. This country is still very far from having high information technology but these materials could be used to create publications that would satisfy the diversified needs of consumers. There are some types of publications that are successful throughout the world but have not yet been developed here: For instance, a magazine like *TV Guide* or a Sunday newspaper.

On Sundays here, when people have more time to read, newspapers do not appear at all because the delivery service has a day off (on Monday there are no newspapers either). Until 1990 newspapers were published on Sundays, but they were not much different from weekday editions. The Sunday newspaper market is nonexistent here, and those who discover it will have a great advantage.

We could also have TV broadcasts from editorial offices, as *The Christian Science Monitor* and *The Wall Street Journal* do, but with our limited number of channels, this idea does not seem to be very promising.

In other words, there are numerous ways to increase the efficiency of the mass media here. And something has been done, but not much. In general, the establishment publications that are not used to independence still prefer to apply to the government for support instead of engaging in commercial activities, where the result is never guaranteed. They are still trying to play the old game because they cannot and will never be able to play the new one. The only real question is how long it will last.

It is evident now that it was naive to expect that the old media could evolve into new ones. It was an illusion of the sort that many people had at the time of early perestroika: that the system could be liberalized and improved without changing its Foundation. The idea was wrong. The totalitarian system could exist only within rigid structures that bounded all spheres of life with no exceptions. Once these structures weakened the whole system collapsed.

It is an illusion to expect that media designed to serve a totalitarian regime could become democratic information outlets. And it is not a matter of ideology, but of a way of doing business. They do not act like independent entities that have nothing but themselves and their readers to rely on. They cannot adapt themselves to the realities of a market economy. They don't seem to realize that in asking the government for support they undermine their independence and professional integrity. The subsidies they receive are like bribes and will have to be repaid by loyalty. They are doomed to extinction.

Only economically independent structures, private ownership of the mass media, sale of information for profit rather than ideological purposes, and efficient utilization of information as a commodity will bring about a real media market.

Approaching all information as a commodity is also necessary to implement modern information technology in this country. The backwardness of the former USSR in this area is devastating and the gap between it and the Western world is increasing every year. Not even the party and state supported media were funded lavishly. High military spending did not leave much for other needs and keeping the media on a strict diet encouraged their obedience. They were given enough money to survive but not to invest in their development.

The results are primitive publishing facilities, backward TV equipment, and a correspondingly low quality of information products. Those who are knowledgeable about the Western media systems find it difficult to believe that only a handful of the largest media here have personal computers. They were the cornerstone of the Communist system. The others still get by with typewriters, and even those primitive machines are not available to every journalist. They write by hand and a typist does the typing.

The same backwardness is typical of the communications system because it was also designed to restrict information and communications rather than promulgate them to the society.

Prospects for direct satellite broadcasting (DBS) do not look good so far. It is unrealistic to expect the quick spread of individual parabolic antennae. The Soviet regulation of DBS made it subject to licensing by Gosteleradio and other state organs. Signals from Western satellites will be available mainly through cable networks. The high price of dishes, as well as their negligible domestic production, will also be obstacles for individual DBS users. The authorities have advocated joint ventures by state controlled or licensed cable operators and Western partners. In any case, they intend to preserve the right to choose what satellite channels viewers are allowed to watch.

In the republics of the Soviet Union, DBS was used to provide an alternative to Central TV and to promote independent exchanges with foreign countries. A satellite relay TV station that is now in operation in Baku allowed Azerbaidjan to receive Turkish TV. The satellite facility was donated by Turkey as a result of increasing political, economic, and cultural ties over the past years.

Telephone communication in the former Soviet Union is unreliable and low in quality. Even seasonal changes influence quality: when it is rainy or snowy, the water often percolates underground and spoils the cable. Because of this problem, in January 1993 all the telephones and faxes in a 5-star Radisson-Slavyanskaya hotel in Moscow did not work for about a week. To have a home telephone installed one needs to wait for several years.

The Soviet military-industrial complex had plans for improving the situation. In 1991, it formed a telecommunications corporation, KOS-KOM, whose task was to upgrade the USSR telephone network. Among the partners were the Soviet space agency Glavkosmos and several defense enterprises. The company had planned to launch twenty-eight satellites within the next three years in order to improve domestic telephone communications. The ultimate goal was to allow any Soviet citizen to place a call by a wireless telephone to any location in the world. But by the end of 1991, both the Soviet Union and Glavkosmos disappeared and the republics will probably have to solve this problem themselves. Their inability to compromise in the Commonwealth of independent states is not an encouraging signal.

The number of lines, especially those going abroad, is now limited. Direct dialing to the West is restricted and calls are usually operator assisted. Ties with the West under perestroika were generally liberalized, but the skyrocketing increase of prices in Russia since 1992 for all government communications services (which have absolutely no competition) early in 1992 was as effective as an iron curtain. The government began sharp increases in prices on January 1, 1992. Prices increased weekly, while salaries went up only once in several months and at a much slower pace. The gap between prices and salaries kept growing, and brought about the impoverishment of wide masses of people. According to Vice President of Russia Alexandr Rutskoy, while at the end of 1991 fifteen percent of the population lived below the level of poverty, by spring 1993 it was sixty percent. The lowest (minimal) level of salaries for state employees (they comprise over ninety percent of labour force), established by the government, could hardly provide for physical survival, let alone mention decent living. Communications, especially with foreign countries, became a luxury. In spring 1992 the lowest monthly salary paid for only a 10-minute telephone call from Moscow to New York, and it took two minimal monthly wages to send an Express Mail letter to the USA. In spring 1993, the salaries, though raised several times, were left still farther back in the race with prices. The increase of the minimum wage to 4500 rubles that was announced in April (but not yet introduced) could cover just 6 minutes talk to New York, and to send an Express Mail letter one had to work for about three months without eating or drinking. An average monthly salary in the country at the same time was 18,000—which does not make much of a difference in terms of consumption of communication services. The Russian government will never admit that it intended to erect barriers to international communications. But it achieved exactly that result by purely economic means. Within Russia prices for telephone communications increased more than a hundred times, damaging even more people. In the other republics, the prices for communication services have also grown but to different levels.

The USSR national program for computerization and information exchange in the country approved in the 1980s failed. Private businesses benefitted from the liberalization of foreign trade and the inability of domestic industries to satisfy the demand for personal computers; they imported them from abroad. But they generally bought them for business and office use. The number of personal computers (PCs) in homes was not really affected by this "invasion" and is still insignificant because the prices of foreign made PCs are prohibitive to most personal buyers. Those produced here are of poor quality and their supply is insufficient.

The construction of computer networks for professional and business use is just beginning. Consumer services like CompuServe and Prodigy are not available at all. It is a vicious circle: services are not being developed because of lack of computers and the number of computers (particularly those in homes) is increasing slowly because of the lack of services.

In general, the information infrastructure in the country is on a very low level. It can't provide for the development of a market economy or satisfy the needs of the emerging civil society or its members. Privatization of at least some sectors of it might stimulate improvement of the whole infrastructure but that is prohibited by the government.

For rapid modernization of the communications infrastructure, it is most important to break the monopoly of the Ministry of Communications. It is now possible to do so within the framework of the Russian government. We do have an advanced communications system in this country: the military's. With the reduction of military spending and number of troops and the conversion of some of the military industry to civil production, there is a real possibility for transfer of some of the military communications resources to the open market. If foreign companies are allowed in this market, they will provide competition that will stimulate the development of the infrastructure. This would also be useful for the military communications industry. Although the quality of their products is high, the military has never been bothered by economic efficiency. Competition in the civilian market will help it get rid of extra fat. A new communications infrastructure will have far-reaching implications for all the directions of development in the country.

It would also be of crucial importance for the introduction of the country to the global communications network because its present structure is incompatible with the world system. As *The New York Times* Bill Keller puts it, this country is only a candidate member in the club of civilized nations.[4] A modern communications network will help to link the former Soviet republics to the world economy.

NEW OPTIONS AND OLD OBSTACLES

Now that most ideological and political barriers to press freedom have been eliminated, the development of the alternative media will depend to a great extent on the new sources of finance to stimulate their development. A strategic goal is to break the still existing dominance of the state and demonopolize the media field.

In the print press and book publishing, where capital investments are not high (to say nothing of publishing facilities), a number of new outlets were financed through sources that were unusual to this country. Among them were legislatures at different levels, independent political and public organizations, cooperatives, joint ventures, private businesses, and citizens.

Though the new periodicals cannot compete with the establishment ones in terms of circulation, they are numerous and mark a very important trend. On the production side of publishing though, the state monopoly has not been challenged. Besides, the names of different associations and foundations listed among the new publishers often conceal state ownership.

During the summer of 1991, Goskompechat was reorganized into the Ministry of Information and Press and made responsible for the registration of the mass media and the "legal protection of national culture from the negative consequences of commercialization of the mass media."

In fact the transformation of the state publishing facilities into pseudo-commercial structures under government control was probably the major goal of the reorganization. Minister Nenashev explained the reorganization as a "necessity to control the market mechanisms on behalf of the state." State publishing organizations were restructured into a number of associations (of book publishers, newspaper publishers, printing plants, and booksellers) and shareholding companies.

Broadcasting property resists demonopolization even more strongly. In theory, many new sources of funding could be used to diversify ownership in the field. But not all of them could exist in the specific conditions of the former Soviet Union. The development of press freedom here is being limited by state politics in communications, which seeks to preserve its dominant position, not to encourage competition.

For instance, government funding that in other countries is generally considered very carefully because of the political interference it can entail is viewed as a proper source of subsidy of technical facilities for the newly created media.

Government funding may sound like an attractive idea for this country, if government really aimed at diversifying the media system. But the present government is very unlikely to do anything of the kind for both political and economic reasons. It is evidently inclined to retain control by the economic and administrative means it now exercises over the media—so why undermine it?

A large source of TV funding is advertising. Even in some West European countries where opposition to advertising is strong, it still goes on the air because of the economic need to sell goods and services and the growing costs of TV production. In the former Soviet Union where the consumer market is depressed, television will not soon become the goldmine it is in countries with prosperous economies. In 1988, Soviet TV received 2.5 billion rubles from the state budget and made only 11 million by itself. Since then, advertising volume and profit have sharply increased but they are still insufficient.

Marketing and advertising are very new business fields in this country. There was almost no need for them in the totalitarian economy, where most goods were centrally distributed. Besides, the consumer market had always been small and producers had no need to compete for consumers.

Now the emerging economy that needs to promote itself has started using advertising. But the art of advertising is unknown and so far the product has been characterized by poor taste and low quality. And from the point of view of the economy, advertising expenditures appear to be absolutely ineffective because they are invested in the wrong media.

The major obstacle to development of advertising as an important source of media income is the collapse of the consumer market. There is no need to spend money on commercials: everything is in short supply and will be bought in any case.

In the late 1980s, the national TV channels that had the most viewers started to make money with commercials that advertised trucks and harvesting machines. Commercial banks and commodity exchanges began selling their shares later: each for a price higher than the life-time income of the average TV viewer. This is economic nonsense but nobody cares. The new advertisers do not act like reasonable business people but nouveau riches who want to let everyone know about their wealth. Target audiences could by reached more precisely and cheaply through business periodicals. The emergence of market competition and the mastering of marketing skills will bring about a redistribution of business advertising among media.

In the countries with a market economy this kind of advertising is far from the most important to the media. Their major source of income is usually consumer advertising and only a market economy can generate enough advertising to satisfy the needs of the media. Therefore, the prosperity of the media is inextricably tied to the general economic situation. Only a flourishing market economy can provide the media economic independence from the government.

Now that the consumer market is weak and there is not enough advertising volume to support the media, sponsorship has also become an important source of funding. But to prevent abuses it is necessary to work out the ethical principles of the relationship between the broadcaster and the sponsor. The principles should provide for independence of programming from the sponsor's influence.

Foreign advertising on Soviet TV is a separate issue. Actually, it became a problem and provoked public controversy from the very beginning. For about a year the trademark of the Italian corporation Olivetti has appeared on the face of the clock that counted the last minutes and seconds before the major national evening news program "Vremya" (Time). It never occurred to TV managers that this was a violation of ethical standards in advertising because there were no standards.

It was not a good deal from the business point of view either. A year-long contract brought in about $1 million. The art of making money by means of Western-style business is pretty new here. And some rules are necessary to regulate it from the ethical and the economic point of view.

The problem of foreign investments in the mass media, especially television, is very sensitive. They could create alternative broadcasting quickly. But, of course, they need some incentives. Businessmen from abroad, including Berlusconi Corporation from Italy, were attracted to Yugoslavia, where about twenty commercial local TV stations already exist, by a liberal law on foreign investments and the low level of taxes.[5] East European countries that do not offer such obvious advantages still invite foreign investments to modernize their backward broadcasting systems.

Foreign investors in the former Soviet Union prefer to enter into joint ventures with the media here rather than investing independently. It helps Western entrepreneurs decrease their levels of risk while operating in a crisis economy in a market very different from theirs.

There are quite a few joint ventures in publishing. McGraw-Hill and Kniga Publishers launched a Russian-language edition of *Business Week*. A French construction group, Bouygues SA, bought a 50 percent share in the French-language edition of *Moscow news*. The magazine *Perspektiva* is published jointly by British Skyset Limited and the Mir publishing house. A U.S. firm, Kombass International Publishing, joined the *Vechernyaya Moskva* daily to start the *Moscow Interbusiness* journal. A Dutch company and the Union of Soviet Journalists began *Moscow Magazine*. The Rodale Press of the United States of America and Vneshtorgizdat publishing house agreed to launch the magazine *Novy fermer* (New farmer). The Hearst Corporation and one of the largest Soviet dailies, *Izvestiya* started a joint weekly newspaper, *We*, in two languages. The *Business Contact Express* bulletin was organized in Leningrad with the participation of an Italian and a German company. *Reader's Digest* is now printed and distributed in Russian jointly with Soviet partners.

The list is long, though far from exhaustive. But there is one peculiarity about it that dampens our enthusiasm. Almost all the joint ventures were organized with state companies, not with concerns that represent other forms of ownership. This is very understandable. From the business point of view, state enterprises are the best partners: they are well established and they have money and guaranteed access to paper resources and printing facilities. All these ventures help diversify the market for periodicals to some extent, but they actually support the state publishing monopoly, not the alternative media.

There is no doubt that most Western partners in joint ventures were guided by business interests. This was not the case with Robert Maxwell, who had been a friend of the Communist leaders since Leonid Brezhnev. He published Brezhnev's books and was awarded an honorary doctorate from Moscow University for it. He also published books by Andropov, Chernenko, Gorbachev, and other East European leaders.

Maxwell could hardly make any money on those books. On the contrary, recently published information indicates that Maxwell's Pergamon Press was among the foreign organizations secretly financed by the Communist party of the Soviet Union.[6]

Maxwell continued his relationship with the Soviet elite during perestroika. In Britain he printed the magazine *Nashe naslediye*, published by the Cultural Foundation, where Raisa Gorbachev was very active. After President Gorbachev retired, the press wrote that *Nashe naslediye* was finished. The magazine was always in the red but its debts were reimbursed from the state budget.[7]

Maxwell Communications became an associate member of the consortium Delovoi mir (Business world) "with special rights" and two seats on its board of directors. The consortium is a business publisher. It was organized by a number of government institutions and headed by Finance Minister Valentin Pavlov who was soon appointed prime minister.[8]

Pravda looked to Maxwell for support after the Communist party was banned.[9]

After Maxwell's mysterious death, his contacts with the KGB became known. He was going to print in Britain an illustrated magazine about the KGB in English and Russian with a circulation of 300,000 copies. After Maxwell's death his heirs refused to finance the project.[10]

Of course Maxwell's enthusiastic support of Communist regimes (in the Soviet Union and Eastern Europe) was unique. But his Western colleagues who were attracted here by purely business interests actually helped old structures survive, instead of promoting the creation of alternatives. Business is business, not charity.

But it is really surprising that charitable institutions sometimes did the same for reasons that are difficult to understand. Soros Foundation awarded a grant for new equipment to Politizdat, the major book publisher of the Communist party.[11] When I asked why a well-established party enterprise was chosen and not some competing publisher, Mr. Soros answered the foundation does not consider the content of what is being published when making grants. The answer did not sound convincing. In Hungary, Soros Foundation supported anti-Communist forces consistently and George Soros' work in undermining totalitarianism in Eastern Europe is widely acknowledged. Because of this background, his grant to Politizdat is really mysterious.

Foreign investors in the audiovisual field couldn't do without government structures if they wanted to. Access to the airwaves is fully controlled by the government. The number of joint ventures is very small and they are limited to music radio: *Nostalgie* and *Europe Plus* with French participation and *Radio maximum* with American.

Although foreign investments should be welcome, they need to be regulated, first with regard to the percentage of a company that a foreign investor can own. This is especially important for TV. Even in the United States, where commercial TV is dominant, a foreigner cannot own more than 25 percent of a TV company. In the European Community, investment in broadcasting companies in the member states is generally permitted with mutual agreements although some countries have stringent restrictions.

The Report of the European Television Task Force indicates that, in general, national laws in Europe concerning foreign investment are more liberal than in the United States. But it stresses that a majority ownership "by non-European shareholders will need to be considered carefully."[12] In the united Europe, neighbors have privileged status and only "non-Europeans" are treated as foreigners. This is a good pattern for the Commonwealth of Independent States to follow.

Still, the question of foreign investment in television is very sensitive. In the present economic situation, about the only thing the government officials can put up to match a partner's investment is a valuable asset like air time. Giving up large amounts of time would actually allow the colonization of the air, especially because most of our programs are not competitive. These issues are outside the framework of television problems; they are political and need to be regulated by law. The "Olivettization" of the "Vremya" program was more than enough.

But there was a possibility that this precedent would be repeated on a much larger scale. In 1990, a preliminary agreement was reached to arrange a joint television venture between the Ministry of Communications of Russia and Berlusconi Corporation: 51 percent was supposed to belong to Russia, 49 to its partner. The Russian government did not then have access to TV broadcasting and was eager to launch republican television. The deal was not completed. But the attempt to make it reflected the conflict of interests between the Center and the republic, which was seeking independence. Russia had the absolute right to have its own television and not just a single channel. But if the contract with Berlusconi were signed, it would challenge the information sovereignty and the cultural identity of Russia.

Now that Russia, since the collapse of the Union, has two TV channels of its own, it does not seem possible that it would be inclined to enter such ventures. Still, it is important to remember the lesson of this failed deal. If the government really intended to encourage commercial television financed by alternative sources (which is doubtful), it could provide tax advantages for them if they reinvested the money in the development of business. But the current tax policies of the Russian government suppress all kinds of business activities. The government could also give credits, but this is not so important now that non-government commercial banks exist.

The problem is that most of the organizations that appear in the broadcasting field now are pseudo-market structures veiling state ownership. By the end of the 1980s when some kind of economic reform became inevitable, ministries and state committees started to reorganize state property under new names such as corporations, associations, and companies. Among them are the Association of Radio and Television formed by Gosteleradio, the Association Radio created by the Ministry of Communications of the USSR, and the Association of Publishers originated by Goskompechat.

The transformation of state publishing facilities into a pseudo-commercial structure was probably the major goal of the reorganization of Goskompechat. They were restructured into commercial state concerns using the technical resources of the state press, printing, and publishing houses, and into associations, one of which was made responsible for consolidation and development of the printing trade in the Soviet Union. The state committee was called a ministry and made responsible for the registration of the mass media and the "legal protection of national culture from the negative consequences of commercialization of the mass media."

The so-called commercial structures in the broadcasting field were all created with the participation of state bodies. This is natural because they are still in command of the economy and have means to invest and the alternative economic structures are still too weak. But what is equally important, there is no legislation in this country to regulate the participation of government agencies and their officials in commercial organizations. The same is true of legislators. It provides foundation for corruption.

An association of commercial television and radio was formed in Kazakhstan. Among its partners were Gosteleradio and the Ministry of Communications of the republic. A deputy minister of communications became one of the two chairmen of the association. Among the members of the association of air, satellite, and cable television were Gosteleradio and the Central Committee of Comsomol, as well as the NIKA TV company organized by it.[13]

The Soviet Cultural Foundation was reported to be creating an independent television company, Telemir (Teleworld), to link twenty-four Russian cities and provide serious competition to Central TV.[14] The report caused some bewilderment. The company was started when the Russian republic could not begin its own broadcasting. One of the excuses for this given by the Union government was lack of resources. It seems that another reason—to use an expression by George Orwell—was so that a "more equal" organization could exist.

We must explain that what are called foundations in the Soviet Union are different from American foundations. They are institutions launched with government money by and for the benefit of people entitled to administer them. Soviet foundations are engaged in commercial activities but enjoy tax deductions as charitable establishments do. In other words, they are institutions designed to support influential people and help them preserve power. The Cultural Foundation enjoyed very special treatment at the top because Raisa Gorbachev was its vice-chairwoman.

The Cultural Foundation was also a partner with the USSR Ministry of Defense and the All-Union Television and Radio Company in the Radar TV Association launched late in 1990 to produce a regular military show for the national network. Deputy Chief of the Main Political Administration of the Soviet Army, Colonel General Grigori Stefanovsky, who was the moderator of the first broadcast, was also in charge of a special project of the Cultural Foundation, "The army and the culture."

In Barnaul, the company TV-Siberia was launched with the Altai Territorial Committee for television and Radio as one of its members. But even such obviously loyal and obedient structures did not last long. The Commercial TV channel Siberia stopped broadcasting after it was on the air for only a few months. As a result of pressure from the territorial party committees, all the channel's sponsors withdrew financial support. The organizers of the channel were, however, optimistic about finding new sources of income since the channel was reportedly very popular with local viewers.[15]

A company formed by the Soviet Defense Ministry was much luckier with the authorities' support. The organization was created to promote positive portrayals of the armed forces in the Soviet media. A company called The Television and Radio Society was designed to make TV and radio programs, as well as video and audio products. The USSR State Committee for Television and Radio Broadcasting was among the cosponsors of the group.

Practically all the new radio stations are partnerships of different organizations. But since the Ministry of Communications controls access to the air, some of its branches are always among the copartners. Thus, Association Radio, which was formed by the Ministry, has a controlling interest in one of the most successful independent stations Echo of Moscow (223,000 rubles out of 377,000 rubles general assets). *Ogonyok* magazine invested 100,000 and the Moscow City Council invested 50,000 rubles. New structures do come into being but the state keeps them under supervision.[16]

The situation is understandable: it is impossible to start anything new in the field without the participation of the organizations that have kept it under their absolute control. Since everything was fully controlled by the state, this is an inevitable transitional stage between a monopoly system and a more pluralistic media system.

But there should be no illusions about the real meaning of what is going on. I would not interpret the participation of state organizations in the commercial entities as indicating an inclination to share power. On the contrary, they diversify their activities in the market economy to preserve and prolong their might.

With generally weakening state power and the collapse of many of its structures people who have access to finance and resources create pseudo-market organizations, formally independent, but based on state property. The goal of the operation is to privatize those companies eventually by selling them to their executives. In the former Soviet Union, where there was hardly any capital outside government control and bureaucracies were numerous and powerful, this road to private ownership became one of the most popular.

"The new democratic power," wrote Vice President of Russia Alexandr Rutskoy,

> will not get prestige, until the ugly tradition of "connection" of political and "commercial" positions is severed. It implies, for example, a state officer, who becomes a board member of a commercial association, bank, company, and so on, and by his "political" activities "contributes" to their financial prosperity.[17]

Neither the state as a whole nor the people who control it are inclined lose their power and ownership. When one of the new Soviet capitalists, Konstantin Borovoi, offered to buy the former Central TV, his offer was decisively rejected.

There is confusion about what's what among the new entities in the TV field here. Western terms can be misleading when applied in such a different context. What is often called commercial television here is programming companies, for example VKT, which was organized by a commercial bank, several commodity exchanges, and other enterprises. It has powerful financial resources behind it and big plans for the creation of a national commercial network. But so far, it only provides weekly programs for Russian TV and the statement of an *Izvestiya* correspondent "Television company VKT is changing the existing world structure of radio and television"[18] is definitely premature. The additional information in the same piece about where and for what price the shares of the company are sold and what its dividends are going to be makes the reader suspect that the newspaper is lobbying for the new enterprise.

Late in 1991, a congress of independent TV companies from five republics of the former USSR gathered in the Ukrainian city of Kharkov. About 150 companies and studios that claimed to have access to 50 million viewers were present. Since access to information is limited and there are many biases on behalf of the news media, it is really difficult to understand what kind of enterprises they are. But there is some information available about the company Tonis, which is considered to be the most successful of all and hosted the meeting. It became popular with the unlicensed presentation of new American movies by rented transmission lines. Its president, Vladimir Ivanenko, has been labeled "the biggest videopirate in the country."[19] The business is definitely evolving but it is still far from being of high standards.

The congress has recognized television programming by commercial companies as their chief goal because it is believed it's likely to lead them to prosperity. Their problem is a lack of TV journalists. The companies plan to receive support from advertisers because the prospects for subscription TV are unclear according to them: the cost of decoding equipment is skyrocketing while the standard of living is declining.

Of course, commercial television and radio are not the only alternatives to the state monopoly. Small public stations, a grassroots kind of broadcasting, will definitely come into being and some facilities are actually ready. I mean the studios in journalism schools here. In American universities, they are often used for teaching students as they are here and as a base for public television stations. We have technology and people in journalism schools who could help broadcasting advance.

We have a number of new video production companies that are independent of the government. Some of their programming is bought by state TV companies; some goes to the foreign markets and is quite successful. This means that TV production from here can be competitive even though most of the existing programming is not. To be marketed internationally, our productions must meet the existing standards for program type, timing, and, of course, quality.

If a market for advanced communications technologies emerges here, it may accelerate the development of alternative media by providing an escape from government controlled structures. For small publications, desktop publishing equipment can provide an independent and economically efficient substitute to the state printing plants. Low-powered TV stations may also help broadcasters avoid dealing on an everyday basis with state organizations.

Cable will also help promote alternatives but it is easier to open new channels than to supply high-quality programming for them. This is also the experience of the countries with advanced telecommunications systems where the number of available channels is greater than can be filled. This country will have to solve both problems at once: building channels and developing programming.

From a formal point of view, prospects for the programming industry look good because the field (unlike broadcasting) is not limited by any regulation or government interference. But the demand of this suddenly widening market for professionals cannot be adequately met in a short time. They were educated in limited numbers to serve just one employee and it will take time to meet the new demand. On the other hand, with a still limited number of broadcasting outlets and cable channels, the programming market will hardly become lucrative immediately.

The state sponsored structures in the mass media of the former Soviet Union have been dominant so far. But they will be able to survive only if they adapt themselves to rapidly changing conditions. So far, they have demonstrated a very low level of adaptability and an inclination to rely on the authorities.

Not only the authorities oppose the diversification of the TV market. However strange it may sound, journalists sometimes resist change, too.

Thus, the Ukrainian television and radio workers appealed to the Supreme Soviet of the republic to establish control over TV. They complained that the republican Ministry of Communications had been leasing TV channels to cooperatives and had drawn up plans to transmit Western programs by republican cable TV systems. Those who signed the appeal believed that the national TV should be protected from foreign domination and that jurisdiction over the republican radio and TV should be handed over to the Supreme Soviet of the Ukraine. Evidently, journalists are no more enthusiastic about the coming competition than officials.

The future of the mass media will be determined by the new structural forms that are appearing as an integral part of the market economy. The beginnings of those forms have already started to appear spontaneously, and they will flourish when a more favorable environment for the media emerges.

The elimination of the ideological and political monopoly of the Communist party, the adoption of the USSR Law on the Press and other news media, the authorization of private ownership, and the secession movements were the major factors in restructuring the mass media in the former Soviet Union. The result of this restructuring is obvious but it could be much more impressive if we had an integrated policy to assist the progress of the entire communications system.

In the modern environment of telecommunication technology, separating one medium from another means breaking the natural ties that connect them into a whole. The approach to the field needs to be changed, as well as the philosophy of the statesmen dealing with it. Our present leaders, raised in the old system, cannot overcome political traditions and cultural customs. First, they are used to departmental isolation in different fields of government. Second, they proceed from the point that everything needs to be regulated, either banned or allowed or restricted and the more detailed the regimentation the better.

But the new generation of politicians will probably understand that the media and communications industries are a united world and that the isolation of one element from the others would be disastrous to the system as a whole. It is impossible to upgrade any part of it while ignoring the rest.

As a second step after recognizing the need for an integral approach, the goals of communications policy should be formulated. Basically, they must be the opposite of those that have been followed since 1917: prohibition, limitation, and restriction of information.

When this country (I am referring primarily to Russia but in the other Commonwealth members the situation is not much different) recognizes the right of its citizens to information as a natural human right and removes all the obstacles to it, this will be the beginning of the end for totalitarianism. The dilemma is this simple: either the government is entitled to provide the people with information it finds adequate and necessary or the people have the right to know. This sounds banal to people in Western democracies but the inheritors of a totalitarian regime still need to discover it. Some kind of regulation of the audiovisual media will be needed, no doubt, but the philosophy behind regulation must consider the new goals of our communication policy.

New economic forces will have to come into being, namely, a new class of owners. For years, the progress in politics has been much faster than that in economics. Most of the problems that have slowed economic reforms are deeply rooted in the homogeneous structure of the lumpen society that is accustomed to equality in poverty. The stratum of the population that has nothing to lose and cannot adapt to the new conditions opposes these changes strongly. Private ownership, which new legislation provides for, will create an economic and social basis for a new stratification of society.

The redistribution of ownership from the state to individuals will bring about a redistribution of authority. A new balance of power will summon new statesmen who will be able to break free of the old mold. They will introduce into politics a notion that will have emerged in the society: that the individual is most important and all human rights and freedoms are his or hers to enjoy. Individuals must be put first not because the state allows it but because it is natural. Freedom of information will be among their most important rights.

NOTES

1. An interview with the Head of the Research and Technology Department of Gosteleradio Valentin Khlebnikov, May 25, 1990. An archive of the author.

2. Oswald H. Ganley, Gladys D. Ganley. *To inform or to control?* The new communications networks. Second edition. Ablex Publishing Corporation. Norwood, N.J., 1989.

3. Stewart Brand. The Media Lab. Inventing the future at MIT. Viking, N.Y., 1987, p. 38.

4. *The New York Times Magazine*, September 23, 1990, p. 34.

5. Stevan Niksic. Foreign Capital in the Yugoslav Mass Media Industries. The European Institute for the Media. Belgrade, 25.06.90, p. 1. (An unpublished paper)

6. *Argumenti i fakti*, No. 42, 1991; No. 49, 1991.

7. *Argumenti i fakti*, No. 50, 1991.

8. *Moscow news*, No. 45, 1990, p. 13.

9. *Moscow news*, No. 36, 1991, p. 4.

10. *Moskovsky komsomolets*, November 9, 1991; December 19, 1991.

11. A presentation of George Soros at the Gannet Foundation Media Center, April 11, 1991.

12. Europe 2000: What kind of television? The Report of the European Tele-

vision Task Force. *Media Monograph No 11*. The European Cultural Foundation. The European Institute for the Media. Manchester, 1988, p. 25.

13. *Izvestiya*, March 22, 1991; Izvestiya, January 6, 1990.

14. *Radio Free Europe/Radio Liberty Daily Report*, March 11, 1991.

15. *Komsomolskaya pravda*, February 7, 1990; *Radio Free Europe/Radio Liberty Daily Report*, March 7, 1991.

16. *Commersant*, No. 16, 1991, p. 9.

17. *Nezavisimaya gazeta*, February 13, 1992.

18. *Izvestiya*, December 26, 1991.

19. *Nezavisimaya gazeta*, December 25, 1991.

5

POST-USSR MEDIA IN RUSSIA: A CASE STUDY

THE UNION IS DEAD; LONG LIVE...

In these days of political instability, economic collapse, social disappointment, and apathy, the situation in the mass media is uncertain. They are flattered by the authorities and manipulated by them in the best Communist tradition. They promote the market economy and appeal to the government to save them from its pressures. They speak for freedom of the press but cannot resist the temptation to identify themselves with the powers that be.

In December of 1991, the Soviet Union ceased to exist. It is no use in speculating whether it was for good or for ill (although most of the consequences have been negative so far). It is just reality. And it is also a turning point in the history of Russia. "The Center," which Yeltsin and his supporters blamed for all the problems of Russia, is gone and so is the Communist party. There is no "war of laws" between the Union authorities and the republics any longer and no "parades of sovereignty," as Michail Gorbachev labeled them.

It happened over a year ago. That's not a long time. But it included a honeymoon for the Yeltsin government with full and uncontrolled power, not limited by any higher authority. However brief the period, the results are worth considering. Yeltsin's victory was formalized in December 1991 by the disintegration of the Union and establishment of the Commonwealth of Independent States (CIS). In fact, he took over from Gorbachev in August 1991 in the aftermath of the putsch.

FROM STATE TV TO STATE TV

Two days after Gorbachev's resignation, Yeltsin signed an edict providing for Russian jurisdiction over the Central (All-Union) TV and radio.

It became the second government controlled broadcasting company in the country after the All-Russian TV and Radio but it was more influential because of its larger audience. This step was expected and foreseeable. What was unusual about it was that the routine procedure of signing the edict was televised. Yeltsin signed it in the same president's office where Gorbachev had announced his resignation forty-eight hours before.

It must have been a demonstration of loyalty to the new master. It was no wonder that the TV authorities found it necessary. Under Gorbachev, Central TV had been openly declared "presidential" and as such, it strongly opposed his nemesis, Yeltsin.

During Gorbachev's last days, the confusion about Central TV became obvious. It is enough to say that it failed to find its own words or the means to praise that great politician who changed the history of this country and the world. In this delicate situation, it could do nothing better than rely on its American colleagues. On the day of resignation after the evening news, Channel 1 broadcast an interview with Gorbachev by CNN Moscow correspondents. On the next night, it showed Ted Koppel's program on the last days of Gorbachev. And that was it.

This visible effort to avoid anything that might displease the new authorities indicated the deep degradation of the system. It was reminiscent of August 1991, when television officials readily obeyed anti-Gorbachev plotters. It was as though history was carrying out an experiment: the political forces involved were diametrically different in these two cases but the reaction of the system was the same.

It was not a matter of political convictions in either case. The spinelessness of TV management was the inevitable result of its total dependence on the state and its lack of freedom.

And there should be no illusion that the transformation of the All-Union State TV and Radio Company into the Russian State TV and Radio Company Ostankino will drastically affect the situation. It is still the same state owned, state funded, and state controlled TV. The only difference is that now it is under the auspices not of the Soviet Union, but of the Russian Federation.

A month later in one of his first interviews to the Soviet press after his resignation, Michail Gorbachev complained that in December 1991, when the Union was declared non-existent and the Commonwealth formed, he found himself in "information isolation." Only a few newspapers made an exception and allowed him to say what he wanted to.[1] The former president was referring to all the media. But TV was the most efficient and influential element in this system of isolation of the leader who was being replaced.

Russian rulers' methods make it highly doubtful that they will actually share control over the former All-Union TV with the other republics. There still existed formal plans for Ostankino to serve not only Russia but the whole Commonwealth of Independent States. Their leaders, including Boris Yeltsin, agreed on it in principle. But it was uncertain whether the agreement will work because there were many differences to overcome: funding, political control, and sharing of air time. The question was whether there was enough goodwill on all sides to overcome these problems.

Only communications ministries of the CIS members have started their joint work promptly because the political disintegration made distribution of frequency the primary need.

The deputy chairman of Ostankino, Eduard Sagalayev, said that "the goal of the new company is to provide common cultural and information space on the territory of the CIS." But he recognized the difficulties of sharing political control of TV between the states and admitted that the company is fully dependent on the Russian government for finance and technology.[2]

In spite of its proclaimed goal, Ostankino covered many events as if "the Center" still existed. Channel 1 sounded like the voice of a higher authority, not just one of several equal member states. It reflected the interests of Russia in conflicts. For instance, its coverage of the conflict with the Ukraine concerning the future of the Black Sea fleet was anti-Ukrainian.

Government pressure was probably a reason for this. Another was the media's tradition of propaganda. Information and plain facts have never been presented as they are. They have always been explained, commented on, and interpreted to fit them into the ideological scheme. The ideology has collapsed but journalists have not yet learned to separate news from views, to be (or at least to try to be) objective and impartial. It is a matter of tradition, a matter of education, and a matter of political culture and custom. In this sense, the new wave in journalism is not much different from the old one. They vary in their political orientation, Communist or anti-Communist, but both defend their cause at the expense of objective information.

There was a question whether the tendency of the heads of states to preserve a "common information space" was strong enough to find a consensus in this area while more immediate military and economic problems that threatened the very existence of the CIS had not been resolved and were becoming more acute.

There was no doubt that the development of an economic union that was a necessity for most of the newly born states would require some common information structures, too. It would be reasonable to make use of those that currently exist. But centrifugal political forces of the former Union are too strong and the consistent destruction or usurpation of the former Union institutions has been an important goal of Russian politics so far.

The Soviet Union died as an entity but it still lives in its inheritors.

They inherited its intolerance, its aspiration to impose its will by means of force on the weaker ones, and its ignorance of human rights. However diversified the politics of individual republics are, they do not make any difference in this particular respect.

In Ukraine, nationalism was used to conserve the old Communist nomenklatura. In Georgia, nationalism had an anti-Communist color. In Russia, old bureaucratic traditions turned out to be much stronger than the proclaimed intentions of the democratic leaders. But regardless of those variations, all of them, and other former republics, resemble each other, like the splinters of one large mirror that used to be the Soviet Union.

This heavy heritage determines and for a long time will keep determining the development of the mass media, too. Its influence is absolutely evident in politics, economics, and lawmaking. But although these influences are external to the mass media, their own behavior bears a distinct mark of the past, too, and exceptions are very rare.

THE PRESS LAW: TO ALLOW OR TO PROHIBIT?

When the CIS was formed, all the laws of the Soviet Union were declared invalid, including the first Law on the Press. The Russian Law on the Mass Media was adopted in the middle of December 1991. It was supposed to go into effect on January 1, 1992, but, because of the controversy that it provoked, the president did not sign it for some time. According to newspaper reports of his meeting with editors, Yeltsin promised to veto the bill.

From the very beginning, the draft law was much more detailed and more regulatory in nature than the Union Law. As one of the authors of the draft, Deputy Minister of the Press and Mass Information of Russia Michail Fedotov explained, "If the Union law was a document of democratic romanticism, the Russian one must become a document of democratic realism."[3] The question is whether a detailed description of what is allowed and what is banned really protects freedom of the press better than the USSR law—not to mention the short and simple "Congress shall make no law . . . ."

However imperfect the draft was, the final version that passed the Supreme Soviet came as a shock for the mass media. The law stated that journalists must disclose their sources of confidential information not only to the court but to investigative officers. Another part of the law actually banned the distribution of video, movie, or photo materials without the permission of all those who happened to be in a sequence or still. On the other hand, the clause that says a journalist is not liable for disclosing a state secret unless he or she obtained information by criminal means was eliminated from the draft.

These amendments and others indicated a tendency to reestablish control over the mass media. What made the tendency still more evident and dangerous was the fact that most of the amendments were proposed by a high-ranking representative of the executive branch: General Procurator of Russia Valentin Stepankov, who at that time was also a member of the Russian legislature.[4]

The failure to separate different branches of government, which was a typical characteristic of the Soviet Union, is potentially ruinous for this rudimentary democracy. Writing laws in their own interests is very convenient for the government bureaucracy and very perilous for a society that is trying to get rid of its totalitarian past.

Most of the controversial amendments that the media and the public strongly protested against, were finally eliminated from the text and the president signed the bill. The law was published in February and immediately put into effect. New publications in Russia were no longer registered according to the Union Law in December after the Russian law was adopted. Registration did not begin again until the law went into effect. But even by March, registration had not yet started because the government was undecided about the amount of the registration fee.

The changes in the law on the Mass Media in the Russian Parliament and some other events (an attempt by the president to merge the Interior Ministry with the KGB that was thwarted by the Constitutional Court is just one example) indicate that the new political leaders don't have democratic values, only a democratic vocabulary that they pragmatically invoke to seize power. If this is really so, the effort to limit press freedom by restrictive legislation was hardly surprising.

The leaders of today treat the media as they were treated in the Communist past: as tools of government politics and ideology that are to be strictly supervised and directed. The last Communist leader of Moscow, Yuri Prokofiev, explained it quite frankly: newspapers and journals that are organs of various government bodies should not be allowed to criticize the Soviet leadership freely (it should be added here that in the Soviet Union all the most influential media were dependent on the government in one way or another). Speaking in February 1991, Prokofiev proposed appointing a special official within the cabinet of ministers to control periodicals of the government. He noted that the CPSU had always had a similar official.[5]

Prokofiev's higher-ranking colleague, the first secretary of the Communist party of Russia, Ivan Polozkov, explained the same position from a more general point of view: "Pluralism may exist on the level of discussions or political movements, but at the state level there must be a single ideology."[6]

One of the politicians of the new wave, Ruslan Khasbulatov, the chairman of the Supreme Soviet of Russia, condemns press conduct and con-

siders it his obligation to teach it lessons in person. Both the manner of
his reprimands and even their wording are very typical of a Communist
leader. At a meeting of the Presidium of the Parliament in January 1992,
he denounced TV Channel 1 because its estimate of the situation in one
of the autonomous republics of the Russian Federation was different from
his own. He strongly disagreed with the media's criticism of the Parliament. And foreign journalists, he added, follow the pattern of their colleagues here. But they would not dare, he thought, do the same in their
own countries with respect to their parliaments. Journalists who cover
Parliament cannot understand the problems being discussed; they are
neither objective nor professional. How can we stand it? he asked.[7]

Of course Khasbulatov can't simply dismiss disagreeable journalists or
editors as his Communist predecessors used to do. But he has some very
effective means at his disposal: he promised to reconsider funding of the
state owned media and the salaries of their staff when the budget was
discussed. In 1992, allocations for culture, arts, and the mass media were
combined in one budget article for the first time. Three months of its
1992 financing was 12 to 13 percent of what was requested. That is 1.2
percent of the budget.

Another target of denunciation by the chairman was the Parliamentary
Committee on the press: "Evidently, our press is arranged in such a way
that we need to regulate it . . . . I do not know what you are doing. But
I do not see your regulatory activities . . . ."

Khasbulatov's conclusion was very serious:

> The mass media are conducting a war against the state . . . . And don't you
> yield to this propaganda about democracy. Remember, how we spoke for
> extending journalists' right to information? But when the state is being
> subverted, it is quite a different matter.

What should the Parliament do about it? "If you think that we are
going to tolerate it, you are making a mistake. There were those who
tolerated, but they went away to nowhere." One of the deputies angrily
retorted that the Presidium should be renamed the Politburo, and Khasbulatov should be called the secretary general.[8]

Suslov, the famous supervisor of Soviet ideology and propaganda under
Brezhnev, can sleep quietly in his coffin: there is still somebody here to
defend his cause and fight against the subversive activities of hostile
propaganda.

Those observations by Khasbulatov on the mass media at the Presidium
of the Russian Parliament were probably the most systematic expression
of his views on the issue but not the only ones.

The tendency to direct, to ban, to supervise, to teach, and to correct
the mass media is very strong. It is not what in Western political vocab-

ulary is called regulation. Although Khasbulatov used this term, what he actually implied was different. No Western politician would dare to humiliate the mass media as Khasbulatov did because they are the fourth branch of government there.

But not here. In this country they have only started toward independence and freedom. New political leaders cannot resist the temptation to use the media for their own ambitions. And they still have enough means to do it, although fewer than their Communist predecessors. Several generations of politicians will have to change before this attitude is overcome.

CENSORSHIP FOR THE BENEFIT OF PRESS FREEDOM

The efforts of the legislature to control the media are not isolated. They are supported by the executive branch of the government. It is typical that in his first TV address to the people after Michail Gorbachev's resignation, Boris Yeltsin could not overcome the temptation to criticize the media.

A presidential edict of January 1992 extended the power of officials to censor the mass media further. To defend the state secrets of Russia, Yeltsin ordered officials "to use as a guide to action the established documents on the issue approved earlier."[9] This implies that all the many regulations that restricted access to information and limited information flow in the Soviet Union can be used anytime. The edict will work for an indefinite period until the adoption of a law on state secrets that will determine what these secrets are. In spring 1993 there is no law yet.

The potential perils of this edict to freedom of information are evident. It also directly contradicts some of the Yeltsin's earlier rulings. In autumn 1991, he ordered the opening of the Communist party and KGB archives that had been closed by a Union regulation. Who is going to decide which of the laws has priority? Evidently, another bureaucrat. And there will be enough of them to do it because Yeltsin ordered that "special separate departments" or "specially appointed people" take care of state secrets.

In September 1991, President Yeltsin issued the edict "About measures for the defense of press freedom in RSFSR."[10] The immediate reason for it was the intention to lift the ban on several publications that were suspended for their support of the August putsch. The edict also ordered the Ministry of the Press and Mass Information "to restore in full volume the principle of press freedom" and it ordered the Council of Ministers "within 10 days to take measures to defend publishing and the mass media in the conditions of transition to the market relations and to solve other issues resulting from this edict."

The idea that ministries can "restore press freedom" or defend the media of the market economy "within 10 days" is rather strange. But there is another point in the edict that clarifies the president's notion of how to defend press freedom: "to create the State Inspectorate for the Defense of Freedom of the Press and Mass Information at the Ministry of Press and Mass Information of the RSFSR."

Regardless of the word *defense* in its title, establishment of the Inspectorate was widely interpreted by public opinion as restoration of censorship. The difference was that, unlike Glavlit, which had been suppressing freedom of the press in this country for seventy years, the Inspectorate censorship was not pre-publication but post-publication censorship.

Later the government made the president's edict concrete. It is significant that the Inspectorate officially aimed at the defense of press freedom was organized like the former Glavlit and its branches. The new institution was entitled to

conduct inspection on the facts of violation of the legislation on the press and mass information;

issue orders for elimination of violations of the legislation on the press and mass information that are obligatory for consideration;

present to the appropriate state bodies materials on facts of violation of the legislation on the press and mass information for bringing to responsibility officials of state agencies, enterprises, organizations, public associations, and also editors (chief editors) of the mass media and citizens;

apply to the institution that has issued a registration certificate for the mass medium or to the court with a statement about termination of the medium's activities on the grounds determined by the legislation on the press and mass information.[11]

By establishing this kind of control over the mass media the Russian administration that gained power under democratic slogans was actually restoring censorship. To give bureaucrats instead of courts the power to determine what is lawful lays the ground work for violations of press freedom that can be implemented as soon as it is needed. And it has already been used.

THE CASE OF *NEZAVISIMAYA GAZETA*

Minister of Press and Mass Information, Michail Poltoranin, (the Inspectorate is a department of his ministry) threatened to close *Nezavisimaya gazeta* (*Independent newspaper*) for publishing an interview with the vice prime minister of the Ukraine, Masik. In the interview he mentioned the possibility of a nuclear attack on the Ukraine by Russia.

The Russian authorities were indignant. But instead of settling the matter with the Ukrainian government by diplomatic means, they directed their anger against the messenger who was luckily within their range of influence, unlike Masik. Poltoranin accused the newspaper of violating the press law (namely, propaganda of war). He warned that if the violation were repeated, *Nezavisimaya gazeta* would be suppressed.[12] As the editor-in-chief of the newspaper, Vitaly Tretyakov, commented, "Democratic leaders follow the footprints of Communist leaders."

Poltoranin typically declared his decision not in an official letter to the editor but in a radio interview. Information about the ministry resolution distributed by the Russian Information Agency was published in the press. An obvious aim was to teach all the media a lesson.

In August 1991, this newspaper and other democratic publications were closed by the putschists. After democracy won, the Russian government was threatening to do the same. This case, regardless of whether the newspaper was right or wrong, reveals all the perils of the bureaucratic control imposed by the Russian president and his administration on the media.

This attempt to tame the press was not accidental. In an extended interview to *Nezavisimaya gazeta*, State Adviser to President Yeltsin, Sergei Stankevich, actually confirmed that it was the policy of the Russian government. He accused the newspaper of sensationalism, unbalanced coverage, and failure to represent different points of view. Behind all these accusations, was the feeling that the mass media had betrayed the government. Yes, Stankevich said, the government "had all the grounds to feel offended.... Offense is not the right word, all the grounds for a protest."[13] If so, why didn't the government bring a suit against the newspaper? First, they knew that there were no grounds for criminal prosecution. Second, going to court to solve conflicts is not customary in this country. The major goal of the government affront was probably to menace the media and make them more manageable.

The new government officials do not and cannot control the media as the Communist government did, but they still expect their allegiance. The officials embrace freedom of the press for as long as the press supports them.

The present Russian government came to power from the opposition, helped and encouraged by the democratic press. And it still wants to enjoy the love and full assistance of the press. It probably doesn't quite realize that the rules of the game have changed. Besides, a Communist mentality that they can't rid themselves of even if they wanted to makes them behave this way.

It's not strange that non-Communist Russian officials often rebuke the press and teach it lessons as their predecessors did. The real difference is that now their power is not as unlimited as it used to be. It may still be sufficient to prevent glasnost from developing into real freedom of the press.

In their attempts to tame the media the authorities do not limit themselves to a threat to suppress publications. After an article, "Poisoned Politics," was published by the *Moscow news* (number 38, 1992), its authors, Vil Mirzayanov and Lev Fedorov, were arrested by the security service and their apartments were searched on the grounds that the article disclosed state secrets. Fedorov was released the same day, and Mirzayanov was kept in prison. The article stated that despite all the declarations by president Yeltsin and other high ranking officials, and despite international agreements signed by Russia, chemical weapons that are more destructive than anything known in this field are still being manufactured and tested. There has been no trial yet.

Whatever the verdict is, the case reveals the vulnerability of journalists facing the state machine. Who determines what is a state secret as soon as there is no law on state secrets? Isn't it the institute, developing the chemical weapons in violation of the official state agreements, that should be put on trial? Shouldn't the officials denounce the information if it is wrong? None of these questions have been formally answered, which reinforced concern about potential for abuse of press freedom by the executive power. This potential still exists in this country, and can become a reality at any moment.

BACK TO AN INFORMATION MONOPOLY

In January 1992, President Yeltsin authorized the merger of TASS and the Russian Information Agency Novosti (RIAN) to form an entity that would serve as "a central state information agency of the Russian Federation." The Ministry of Press and Mass Information were its authors. Officially, the move was justified mainly by budget considerations. But there was a more important motive for the Russian leaders to encourage the merger: it monopolized information sources (officially it was called eliminating duplication of activities) and got rid of the current management.

RIAN antagonized the Russian government by distributing economic information on freezing of bank accounts and the suspension by Russian banks of all cash payments except salaries. The information referred to unnamed sources in banks and was not officially confirmed. The government was so irritated by its publication that Vice Prime Minister Yegor Gaidar ordered the Agency of Federal Security (AFS) (the Russian KGB) to conduct an investigation to find the source of the information. The document with the results of the investigation was signed by the general director of the AFS, V. Ivanenko. The report, which was addressed directly to Gaidar, was leaked to the press.[14] It deserves special attention as a confidential document that uncovers the real attitudes to the mass media at the highest level.

The AFS complained that the management of the information agency did not reveal its sources; it referred to the law on the press and other news media. The published information was not based on the government documents RIAN was provided. At the same time, the document stressed, "even a cursory analysis of the Russian press" reveals that there was a leak of information from the government. One newspaper mentioned specifically was *Kuranti*, which published material of the same kind that the RIAN distributed and whose author also refused to disclose his source.

What the document did not say but definitely implied was that the RIAN information, although unconfirmed, was correct. But the leak and the reaction to it made the government change its plans. Otherwise, it would be impossible to explain the angry reaction and appeal to the security service.

The Agency of Federal Security considered it necessary to attract the attention of Minister of Press and Mass Information Poltoranin to the fact that "unjustified tendency of some journalists to sensationalism, publishing of unverified materials leading to destabilization in the society, may become a source of dissatisfaction of the population with unpredictable consequences." The document stressed the need to enhance the journalists' "personal responsibility" for the accuracy of the data they used. The document strongly demanded that the government reduce the number of cases where unverified materials were published by using the law that guarantees non-disclosure of information sources.

Those publications can play "a provocative role," the general director of the AFS warned. He did not rule out the "premeditative character" of those activities among some journalists and promised that the security service would "carry on preventive operations with them."

It is difficult to believe that this document was dated December 1991, but it was. "Provocative role" and "preventive measures" definitely come from the old vocabulary that the KGB used in its struggle against dissidents. This intolerance in the government of anything that it considers disloyal is typical of the Communist regime, too.

But the very fact that leaks occurred demonstrates that times have changed. Once RIAN could not distribute information that was not officially confirmed and approved. And the publication of an internal document of the government from the KGB would have been absolutely impossible, too. These events prove that the process of change, however slow and difficult, is continuing despite the resistance of the old system.

That resistance is really strong. Other confirmation of it is an open letter of the editor of *Kuranti*, Anatoly Pankov, to the general director of the AFS. Rejecting the security service condemnation that the newspaper had published information "in provocative means," the editor accused the AFS of tapping his home telephone and those in the editorial office. He demanded an investigation and an official response.[15]

The conflict between the government and some of the media was obviously quite sharp. The government could not take any direct actions against *Kuranti* because it did not control the paper. But the state agency RIAN was another matter.

No specific criticism was leveled against another object of the merger, TASS. But it was an old Union structure; for the Russian government, that was more than enough reason to reshuffle it.

The story of this merger also reveals the inconsistency of the politics of the Russian government and publicizes behind-the-scenes struggles. There are many strange occurrences in politics today but this case looks special. On the morning of January 22, Minister Poltoranin announced to the Committee for Press of the Supreme Soviet that on January 20 the president had signed an edict merging the two agencies into one, RITA. Deputies spoke against it, as did journalists from both agencies. Several hours later Poltoranin personally telephoned editors of the major media to say that the edict had not been signed yet but was being considered.

This strange inconsistency provoked speculations about its motive. Some newspapers supposed that the aim of the first announcement was to probe public reaction and when it turned out to be unfavorable, Poltoranin backed down. But that was hardly so, because a new announcement, two days later, was basically the same. It was dated January 22, not January 20 as before. The name of the new entity was changed too: not RITA, but ITAR. To preserve its market, it would sell information under the trademark ITAR-TASS.

Again, as in the case of Central TV it was declared that the edict "does not mean to take over TASS and deprive former republics of communication channels." On the contrary, Poltoranin said, TASS must work to unite sovereign states.[16] It certainly would, but as a Russian agency, not an interrepublican one.

The Russian government is either misleading the public or hallucinating. Having taken over an All-Union organization, it declared that it would serve all the republics as in the past. But how? Will the new sovereign states participate in financing? Will those states share political control, as is inevitable in a state agency? And how are they going to cover conflicts between the states? The Russian government has already demonstrated that it cannot be tolerant enough to the neighboring countries. They have done the same.

ITAR will serve the former republics, but it will do so as any world news agency does—gathering and selling information regardless of state borders. Direct control by the Russian government of the organization excludes other possibilities.

There are also economic reasons that might have encouraged the government in this merger. To justify the deal, Poltoranin said that RIAN asked for too much money. Actually, the agency did not ask for funding;

it already had sponsors who were interested in investing but not if it were a state controlled structure. RIAN planned to go public and decrease the share of state ownership. This would enable the agency to become self-sufficient. In theory, the government should be pleased. But the ultimate result would be a loss of control that the government could not allow.

The financial situation of debt ridden TASS radically improved as a result of widening commercial activities. By the end of 1991, it made a profit. Economic prosperity might create political independence because the Soviet Union, which owned TASS, collapsed. But Russia took the agency under its jurisdiction to ensure political control.

This government, which complains about the huge budget deficit and excessive spending, is not interested in the economic efficiency of state information structures. Profitability would give these organizations independence, but that is the last thing the government wants. The state prefers to subsidize them from the budget, or in other words, to keep them on their knees and not allow them to make the money that would give them freedom and independence.

And it is not only information organizations (because of their propaganda potential) or state organizations that are treated this way by the Russian government. Its attitude toward independent business concerns is basically the same: it tries to keep them under bureaucratic control and financial pressure so they won't be fully independent of the government.

Several months later, the TV equipment of the former RIAN was transferred to Russian television. Thus the merger also eliminated the very vague prospect of competition against one more state monopoly, that of TV.

This reorganization, wrote the editor-in-chief of *Rossiya*, Alexandr Drozdov, "may really create a new climate for the Russian press."[17]

The merger was criticized by the mass media and the legislature. In his interview in *Nezavisimaya gazeta*, Chairman of the Committee on the Mass Media Vyacheslav Bragin strongly condemned the "unworthy and disrespectful to the Supreme Soviet" practices of Yeltsin's administration in restructuring the most important state information institutions.[18] He considered that the reorganization of the All-Union TV and Radio into Ostankino and the merger of RIAN and TASS violated the rights of the Parliament.

The committee sent a formal letter to the president demanding that he adhere to legal procedures in the mass media field. In particular, it demanded that he postpone the signing of the edict on the merger so the committee could appoint specialists to study it. The committee chairman spoke against the formation of a "new monopolism" in the information sphere and the creation of an "information monster." If the edict was signed, the committee planned to appeal to the Supreme Soviet to suspend it.

The opposition of the committee did not prevent the signing of the edict and the intention to suspend it has never been realized.

ECONOMIC PRESSURES

The economic situation does not look promising for the media either. Skyrocketing costs of newsprint, production, and distribution and falling circulations are a heavy burden for all publications. It is not only inflation that is to blame for the growing costs but also the continuing dominance of state monopolies in virtually all sectors.

A recent example was the attempt of the Ministry of Communication to raise delivery prices 400 to 500 percent because of increased transportation prices. The increase was announced late in 1991 after the subscription campaign for the next year was completed. If the newspapers had to cover the new delivery prices, an annual subscription would pay for only several months of costs.

The general outcry of the press made the Ministry of Communications postpone the increase. The 1992 ministry losses for home and office delivery were to be covered by a government subsidy. But this subsidy did not mean that all the newspapers would survive until the end of the year. Hyperinflation swallowed the subsidy rapidly.

With the rapidly growing newsprint prices, nobody knew what newsprint would cost in several months and whether the subsidy would be enough to cover it. In the first month of 1992, about twenty newspapers and magazines became bankrupt; among them were publications of the deceased Union and independent publications.

The newsstand sales of newspapers had already been disastrously affected early in 1992. The national distribution agency Rospechat demanded that newspapers increase their cover price 400 to 500 percent. The agency adds 25 percent to that amount; that means that the more expensive a publication is, the better it is for the agency. But this increase raised the prices of dailies to the level of weekly or monthly magazines and resulted in a loss of readers.

By the beginning of February when the new rates were to be imposed, some newspapers reported temporary suspension of newsstand sales and started looking for alternatives, including direct contacts with regional distribution services.[19] If they were successful, Rospechat would suffer huge losses. A year later, by spring 1993, no serious alternatives had appeared yet, and Rospechat periodically increases rates, enjoying its monopoly.

In any case, further drops in circulations and more bankruptcies of periodicals are inevitable. But the most serious result will be the fragmentation and regionalization of the traditional press system. National newspapers, which serve the entire country, will fail to do so because of the prohibitive distribution costs of covering this huge territory or because the number of subscribers will be too small to exercise national influence. Besides, the increase of newsprint prices is threatening to turn their greatest advantage, high circulation, into an unbearable burden.

In fact, this process has already started. First, the disintegration of the Union turned national newspapers into primarily Russian papers, although they still had some subscribers in the former republics. Second, while establishment national newspapers are losing readers the new publications are gaining them. The trend continued through 1992-spring 1993. But the distribution of those newcomers is inevitably limited; in fact, most have a local character. Nationalism is also stimulating those trends.

Although the independent press is on the rise, the traditional press is more competitive for reasons originating in the old economic system. Establishment newspapers and periodicals, regardless of their present affiliation, have been and are printed at the publishing facilities of the Communist party and the state. They have huge publishing houses behind them that can help them solve supply and production problems. Their editorial offices are situated in the buildings of those publishing houses.

After the August putsch when the Communist party collapsed, the democratic publications favorable to the new authorities received access to printing facilities, distribution, and so on. The ones that they controlled were treated best. The new power inherited the privileges of the old one that it had opposed. When the Ministry of Communication was going to raise delivery prices, the government originally responded to the general demand to help the press by agreeing to subsidize some newspapers—those it controlled.

In February 1992, President Yeltsin's edict announced a higher scale of newspaper subsidies, but they could not satisfy all the publications that needed help. The question is, how is the government going to select the neediest? The answer is, on purely political grounds. *Pravda* and the other newspapers that used to be published by the Communist party were left without subventions.

President Yeltsin presented the Ministry of Press and Mass Information with one of the best and most modern office buildings in Moscow, occupied until recently by the Council of Ministers of the USSR, the Press Building, which is supposed to provide offices for some of the new media. It is not difficult to guess what kind of "independent" press will be selected to staff this building—loyal and obedient.

Some think this step is intended to improve the relationship of the president with the press. Cynics (or realists?) call it a bribe. Still others interpret it as a special award to Poltoranin, who supported Yeltsin at different stages of his political career. He worked to organize support of the media when Yeltsin was in opposition and in power. This is very possible because Poltoranin's rank in the government was raised to vice prime minister at about the same time. In any case it is impossible to explain why this very expensive building, equipped with the most sophisticated security systems to protect it from electronic intelligence, was used to house editorial offices.

Since all supplies are limited, any kind of affiliation of newspapers with the power structures ensures the most favorable treatment because almost all the means of production are still state owned.

This means that opposition and uncommitted publications will face unfair competition although they are not restricted or persecuted for ideological or political reasons.

The prices of newspapers published by the Russian government are half those of the others. They have the best facilities and offices. And it is not just a few of these newspapers but a whole system of them.

Having come to power, the Russian authorities did their best to reproduce a press system like that of the old Union except that it couldn't be as global and universal. They control news agencies and the newspapers of the government and the legislature. The Ministry of Press and Mass Information has also founded a number of regional and youth newspapers. This fact has not been widely publicized and their exact number is not known, but there are figures that give some idea of how wide the government propaganda activities are.

For financing the media the Committee of the Supreme Soviet of Russia requested 5 billion rubles for the first three months of 1992, including 70 million for the newspapers published by the highest state institutions, 700 million for the regional and youth papers, 225 million for TASS and RIAN, 200 million for book publishing, and 3 billion for broadcasting.[20] The actual funding was much lower: only 6 billion rubles for the media and culture and arts. Later on additional subsidies were allocated to keep the press going.

Under the Communist regime there were no other media than those the power structures controlled and subsidized (and sometimes made profits on). But now that some alternatives do exist, why should taxpayers support this system of government propaganda instead of paying directly for what they like?

In broadcasting, the hegemony of the state is even more clearly defined than in the press. The national TV channels that used to be under Union control are supervised by the Russian government. All the means of distribution (transmitters, receivers, satellites) belong to the Ministry of Communications.

A number of new radio stations appeared in the last years. Many of them are joint ventures with foreign companies. They have a limited broadcasting zone and cannot compete with the national networks. The best known is the Echo of Moscow, which is a popular alternative news source for the metropolitan area. It is typical, that with the exception of the Echo of Moscow, all the new new radio stations that declare themselves independent have their offices and studios in the Gosteleradio building, where the state broadcasting originates from.

According to Union rules, only ministries or other state bodies that own radio stations can apply for frequencies. This means that at least one partner in all these companies is the state and it controls the most crucial aspect—technical access to the airwaves.

The Russian government can change the rules, of course. But its actions so far, in both politics and economics, have not been encouraging. The Russian regulations on property adopted in January 1992 directly prohibited privatizing television and radio centers and the communications infrastructure. As a result, state TV and radio will continue to be dominant in this country with only a vague prospect of other participants, at least under the present legislation.

There is a trend toward the construction of small cable systems throughout the country. But there is no programming for them and they generally show unlicensed videos and movies.

The climate for the development of freedom of the press does not look very good. Michail Gorbachev, who did so much to liberate it, criticized the "pernicious attempt" of the Russian government "to make the press more obedient."[21] There is no direct repression of the press so far but the potential is obvious. Both the legislature and the executive branch are threats. The collapse of the economy and growing tension in the society create a serious threat of actual repression.

The limitation of information that has lasted since Communist rule is another threat to the freedom of the press. "To get full information is as difficult for us now as it was in time of the CPSU," wrote *Kuranty* editor Anatoly Pankov.[22]

The present democratic government does what its Communist predecessors never did: it sells information to foreign journalists for hard currency, ignoring the national media. Russian Procurator Valentin Stepankov, who was in charge of the investigation of the August putsch, refused to give any information to the media here but supplied it, including video materials, to BBC, *Time*, *Bild*, *Spigel*, and others for a fee. He started doing this on August 26, 1991, several days after the putsch. As a result, the foreign public was better informed about the investigation than our people were. The Procuracy received money but cannot justify the way the government executive handled the official information.

The Foreign press enjoys priority treatment from many government institutions. Not only today's news, but also secret information from the Soviet archive that is now being declassified is sold for foreign currency. The Russian audience gets this information via foreign news agencies or

TV companies. Media professionals here fairly criticize this practice. And some foreign correspondents, whose newspapers' codes of ethics prohibit them to pay for information, are also unhappy about it.

It was only an illusion that we could become free as soon as Communism fell. The old power structures collapsed. But those that replaced them grew up in the same soil, digested the same stereotypes and modes of behavior, and now reproduce them, maybe unwillingly. The same is true of the media and the society as a whole.

Developing a free media system is difficult work that will take a long time. We are at the very beginning of it. It is a challenging task for politicians, for the media, and for all the society. There will be no miracles. Just long, hard work.

Political developments of late 1992 and early 1993 provide no basis for a more optimistic prognosis. Out of a long list of events that illustrate the increasing trend of the authorities to control information, I'll take the most typical and impressive ones.

In December 1992, President Yeltsin created a Federal Information Center of Russia (FIC). Its goal is to supervise the activities of the government media, including television and TASS. Michail Poltoranin, first vice prime minister, who is responsible not to the prime minister, but directly to the president, was appointed to head it. Evidently, the new structure provides for a more strict control over information. It is no wonder that journalists of different political platforms immediately started calling the FIC the "Ministry of Propaganda" that it really is.

Poltoranin did not even care to mask propaganda goals of the FIC. In his interview with *Izvestiya* he said: "We handle the state system, and the fourth branch of government must help us in it."[23]

The idea of FIC has been discussed since spring 1992, but it was not realized until December, when Yeltsin proposed a national referendum for April 1993. At that moment the new powerful propaganda machine started operation.

TV has experienced several reorganizations and shifts in management. In November 1992, Yeltsin dismissed Chairman of Ostankino, Yegor Yakovlev. In January 1993, the company got a new director, Vyacheslav Bragin. As in the case of Poltoranin, it was a purely political appointment for the purposes of conducting pro-president propaganda. Bragin used to be a secretary of a district party committee in the city of Tver; later he was elected a member of the Supreme Soviet of Russia and head of the Committee of the Supreme Soviet on the mass media. In one of his first interviews as the head of Ostankino, Bragin commented on his appointment in this way: "We tread on the tail of the pro-Gorbachev, anti-presidential team, and didn't allow them to do things the way they used to here."[24]

The political character of the appointment was stressed by a quick organization of a special department under the chairman. Officially it was supposed to take care of political pluralism in Ostankino programs. But considering the fact that the head of the department, Kirill Ignatyev, belongs to the management of the Democratic Russia Movement, the impartiality of his department is highly questionable.

Another action by the president was issuing a decree that raised the status of the Russian TV Channel 4 (educational), which it used to share with Ostankino. It was fully transferred to Russian TV, along with some other resources. More importantly, the edict ordered the Ministry of Communications and Russian TV to develop a broadcasting network that will provide for a "maximum coverage of the population of the Russian Federation."[25]

In Russia it is the government, due to its command of finance and material resources, that has the means to control or influence most of the media. Those media are widely used by the government and the president in their propaganda against the Supreme Soviet. It is no wonder that the latter has made a number of attempts to widen its own influence over the press and TV. In March 1993 the struggle between the government and legislature for control over the mass media took the form of a direct confrontation. The abortive attempt by the president to establish a regime of a special rule on March 20 was accompanied by a decree "about defense of the freedom of mass information." In response, the 9th Congress of people's deputies adopted a resolution "about measures aimed to provide for press freedom on state TV and radio broadcasting and in information services." Irrespective of the concrete details of those documents, the clash itself is an evident demonstration that the existing law on the press does not defend its freedom. And whoever declares himself a guarantor of press freedom can easily abuse it.

The law is also used by the Ministry of Press and Mass Information to persecute Communist and nationalist publications. Thus, in March 1993, the ministry started law suits against the newspapers *Den* and *Sovetskaya Rossiya*, demanding their closure for alleged violations of the press law. Though it hardly seems possible that the ministry will win, attempts to silence political opponents under this government will definitely continue. Another recent example is a suspension of "600 seconds," a TV program.

Since Michail Poltoranin left the ministry for the Federal Information Center, it has been headed by Michail Fedotov. Like the president, who declared his wish to defend the media, Fedotov after his appointment announced that the ministry must defend the press, and that as a result, it would defend the society from those who violate press law. He especially stressed the role of the inspectorate on defense of freedom of the press and information.[26]

There are numerous means the powers that be can and do use to influence the media. Many are used all over the world in some form, but others seem to be unique. In January 1993 the chairman of the Russian union of journalists, Vsevolod Bogdanov, in an interview to *Komsomolskaya pravda* mentioned creation of a "journalists' bank". He didn't mean data bank, as the term might suggest, but rather a financial institution with capital of 250 million rubles. It is supposed to support journalists, media, and different projects in the field. That sounds good, except for the fact that the largest shareholder of the bank is the state. When asked, "How are you going to arrange your relationship with the state structures that deal with the problems of the press?" Bogdanov answered: "I am not sure I'll be able to gain impressive victories if I struggle against them."[27]

A chairman of a professional organization is supposed to defend the interests of its members and confront the authorities whenever it is necessary to achieve this goal. Personally, as a member of the union of journalists, I feel my interests to be betrayed by the chairman answering this way. I guess his answer illustrates the longevity of the old Communist tradition in the journalists' organization. Within Soviet history it was headed by the editor-in-chief of *Pravda*, and the real goal of the union was not to defend its members, but to promote party policy and ideology through them. There is no Communist party to obey any longer, but there is no tradition of opposing the authorities either. The interview is entitled: "Can the power hold its ground by using pens?" The answer is: yes, at least for a while; probably, for a long while.

NOTES

1. *Komsomolskaya pravda*, February 1, 1992.
2. *Nezavisimaya gazeta*, January 11, 1992.
3. *Komsomolskaya pravda*, November 28, 1991.
4. *Izvestiya*, December 23, 1991.
5. *Radio Free Europe/Radio Liberty Daily Report*, February 6, 1991.
6. *Radio Free Europe/Radio Liberty Daily Report*, March 7, 1991.
7. *Izvestiya*, January 21, 1992.
8. *Moskovsky komsomolets*, January 21, 1992.
9. *Moscow news*, No 5, 1992, p. 17.
10. *Sovetskaya Rossiya*, September 14, 1991.
11. *Rossiiskiye vesti*, No. 26, 1991.
12. *Nezavisimaya gazeta*, October 30, 1991.
13. *Nezavisimaya gazeta*, October 31, 1991.
14. *Kuranti*, January 29, 1992; *Nezavisimaya gazeta*, January 29, 1992.
15. *Kuranti*, January 29, 1992.
16. *Izvestiya*, January 24, 1992.
17. *Rossiya*, No. 5, 1992.
18. *Nezavisimaya gazeta*, January 24, 1992.

19. *Komsomolskaya pravda*, February 1, 1992; Izvestiya, January 31, 1992.
20. *Rossiya*, No. 5, 1992.
21. *Komsomolskaya pravda*, February 1, 1992.
22. *Kuranti*, January 29, 1992.
23. *Izvestiya*, December 28, 1992.
24. *Rossiiskaya gazeta*, March 3, 1993.
25. *Rossiiskaya gazeta*, January 29, 1993.
26. *Izvestiya*, December 28, 1992.
27. *Komsomolskaya pravda*, January 12, 1993.

CONCLUSION

In the beginning of this book, I considered the idea that the Soviet media structure and the system as a whole could evolve to a new level. This was the illusion that the founder of perestroika, Michail Gorbachev, had about the society as a whole. He had the idea of bringing the Soviet Union back into the community of civilized countries by reforming socialism.

But illusion clashed with reality. The Soviet system was unreformable. Its basic principles, values, and structures could not adapt to new conditions because they were not only different from those of the civilized world but contradictory to them. Soviet-style totalitarianism, by its nature, could not develop into democracy. The Soviet media's problems are not different from those of the whole country: their diseases are the diseases of the entire system.

Communist totalitarianism embraced all of reality including mass and individual psychology and thought. It was a way of life, a way of thinking, and a way of feeling. That is why liberation from it has been such a long and agonizing process. The state, which finds it natural to control everything and resists losing its privileges is not the only problem. There are also the people who take this control for granted. Since 1985, perestroika has been a painful work of demolishing the old forms and the old structures. But this positive movement is just the beginning and has been very weak so far.

The first and most important lesson of perestroika in the mass media is that there can be no genuine freedom of the press in a country with a state controlled economy. Legislation that provides for freedom of the press is essential. It exists now but it will be only theory without the economic structures to make it workable.

This country will never be able to get rid of Communist totalitarianism as long as state ownership prevails, as it still does. For generations, people in this country have been deprived of economic freedom, of the right to private ownership. At this point, economic freedom is the only way that people will become equal to the state and independent of it. Without it neither the market economy, nor an effective democracy, nor guaranteed human rights will be possible.

Private ownership is the most important factor for the development of a free press in this country. I don't mean only in the media (that will come by itself) but, first of all, in the economy as a whole. The separation of economic power from political power is an imperative.

The country is living in a transitional period between two systems. The processes in the media are very complicated and contradictory. The state structures still dominant in the mass media simulate a transformation into independent commercial entities by changing labels and reorganizing. Masks are used to present state owned institutions as pseudo-market institutions or as institutions that are developing in this direction.

This mimicry creates an appearance of redistribution of ownership that may mislead a superficial observer. Scrupulous analysis of the processes of the mass media is needed to understand what is actually going on there, in order not to confuse semblance for essence.

Movement to a market economy has begun. The country is past the point of no return. It cannot be stopped on its road from socialism to capitalism. As Michail Gorbachev used to say, the process has started.

The question is what kind of capitalism the country is moving toward. It is difficult to deceive history, so the low level of economic, political, and social development of this huge country makes it probable that it will ultimately resemble the capitalism of the nineteenth century. In fact, the present course of economic reforms of the Russian government is moving in that direction. The number of paupers quickly increases to a dangerously high level, while the middle class, which stabilizes the system in the other nations, is very small and is decreasing. Private ownership is not encouraged. This situation raises the possibility of a social explosion. This explosion could result in the restoration of some kind of dictatorship in the former Soviet Union because of its heavy social inheritance.

Now as a new society is being built, the mass media can play a crucial role again as they did at the start of perestroika. They cannot do it with the unlimited support of the government; on the contrary, they must be a counterbalance to government, a separate power. But this cannot be achieved quickly. They can do it by illustrating the values that Western civilization is based on and by explaining to the people the kind of society they will gain through their sacrifices. This would also help to defuse the potential for social explosion. But the present media with few exceptions can't do it efficiently enough because they were designed for a very different system and the new ideas are not natural to them.

However pressing the economic conditions are, it is very important to make special efforts to develop the mass media system before the other institutions of the society. Michail Gorbachev managed to do this when he started his reforms and, as a result, he provided a powerful stimulus to all the other innovations.

The present political leaders will hardly be able to do anything of this kind in post-perestroika and post-USSR Russia. On the contrary, they are interested in preserving as much state control over the media system as possible; only a new vision can promote new values.

At present, the militant pro-government propaganda works not only against the government and the media, but also against the general course of political reform. The media cannot get out of the vicious circle of conformity, loyalty and obedience. What is worse, the media reflect the traditional way of thinking in Russian society, whether under monarchy or under communists, instead of trying to break this stereotype. Russia is used to an authoritarian way of rule. Politics has been always personified in one leader, whether he was called tsar, secretary general, or president. In mass conciousness, the tsar has always been a symbol of fairness and kindness, while all the troubles of the people were attributed to malicious landowners. Under the communist regime, propaganda made of Lenin and Stalin symbolic leaders like a tsar. It is worth mentioning that people did not attribute mass repression under Stalin to the leader himself—to the majority he seemed to be irreproachable.

After Stalin, the brainwashing system ceased to work as well—what was a tragedy has become a farce. Nevertheless, the inclination to rely on a strong leader has remained one of the principal characteristics of the Russian people. This might have been one of the deepest reasons for the low popularity of Michail Gorbachev in his last years in power: after a long line of authoritarian leaders he, who rejected their mode of doing politics, seemed to be weak. It was absolutely unfair, of course, because to break totalitarian tradition the way he did took much more courage than to keep it going.

Yeltsin was much closer to the people's stereotype of a leader: he was charismatic and seemed to be strong. He fit well in the system of political values of the majority of the nation.

On the other hand, this majority does not quite understand the role of the parliament. Under the Communists, Soviets of People's Deputies were puppet organizations whose role was to stamp the Communist party decisions by a unanimous vote. There was no separation of powers, and government officials were at the same time members of legislatures.

The present Russian legislature, good or bad, is the first in the history of the country that is trying to make its own policy, independent of the executive branch. On the other hand, all the experience of the president as a high ranking Communist party apparatchik has taught him that he should not expect any disobedience, even less opposition, from the legislature. The president could not take the parliament's independence as natural; he couldn't even submit to this fact. The president declared war on the parliament.

The war was easier for him, because for the general public the role of a parliament was unclear. It was a new institution, strange to the Russian mentality, while the role of the leader was clear—it was he who was supposed to guarantee stability, prosperity, and so on. That is why anti-parliamentarian actions of the president, which in a democratic society would be rejected, often meet with understanding and public sympathy here.

It's a mysterious fact, but according to opinion polls, many more people support the president than approve of his politics. Their support seems more emotional than rational: He is the one to whom an average citizen hopes to shift his or her burdens and responsibilities. This reliance on a leader is typical for a totalitarian society, not for a democratic one.

In 1992-1993, the conflict between the president and the legislature has become a very serious test for the mass media in this country who call themselves democratic, and who they failed to pass. What they had to do was to promote the idea that there can be no democracy without a representative power, and that to fight parliament means to fight democracy.

Instead, pro-government media (the majority of all the media in Russia) promoted and cultivated anti-parliament sentiments. They advocated the idea that the way to democracy is through the strengthening of the personal power of the primary leader—through authoritarianism. Well, if that were so, there would hardly have been a more democratic country in the entire world than Russia. Nobody's totalitarian experience has been as long as ours.

By this kind of propaganda the media slow down the process of democratization. They support the tradition of authoritarian policy, personified in one leader, and do their best to prove that there are no alternatives to Yeltsin. They have a short memory: just about a year and a half ago most of them said that there was no alternative to Gorbachev. There are no alternatives in a totalitarian society. In democracy, there is always an alternative.

Thus, objectively, the establishment media in Russia are now playing an anti-reformist role, as opposed to being one of the engines of reform as in the years of perestroika.

The emerging business class will most probably become the bearer and promoter of the new attitudes and new expectations to the media. This social stratum is more interested in the development of a market economy and political democracy than the others. For this reason, it is the most adaptable to Western values. These people are learning them for purely pragmatic reasons. When in Rome, do what the Romans do. If you're a newcomer in the world business community, learn to play by to its rules.

To improve the business environment here, they must make sure that those basic values that are new into this country become familiar and acceptable. The opening of the country to the global channels of mass communications is the quickest and the most efficient method for achieving this. These channels will present Western culture, values, and ethical norms to the post-Communist society, helping it to adapt itself to the new conditions.

It is evident that Russia will enter the twenty-first century in its own way. It will not be like the Swedish, American, or Japanese model. In general, though, it will share some of the same economic, social, and political values and freedoms. It is a challenging task to develop a new media system based on these values and promote them. Our beginnings have been very weak and uncertain. That is why various forms of international assistance may be of great help. The mass media, think tanks, and charitable foundations of the developed countries could lend their expertise and resources to support the free press here.

In this transitional period between the two systems, the processes in the media are highly complex and contradictory. In this ambiguous situation, it is not easy to figure out a really effective way to stimulate the development of independent media. To be efficient, this assistance needs to be based on a thorough understanding of the processes occurring here.

It is important to know politicians' and government executives' points of view. But this is only a part of the information necessary for choosing rational ways to promote the development of the free press. The widest possible range of information sources should be used to provide the best reflection of reality.

The Freedom Forum's (former Gannett Foundation's) approach to the issue can provide a model. The most important aim of forum activities is to promote press freedom in Russia and other former Communist countries by funding research, conferences, different kinds of programs, and so on. The forum does this after a thorough study of the media issues in the countries involved. The trustees and officers of the forum traveled to Russia to study the problem on the spot. To estimate the state of the media, the delegation did its best to gather information from the widest possible range of sources: the mass media, politicians, independent researchers, state educational institutions, and opinion polling. As a result, the forum obtained a very comprehensive picture. They are in a position now to make expert decisions about measures that can assist this country in the formation of a free mass media system.

This assistance is needed very badly. A recent statement by the chairman of the Russian legislature, Ruslan Khasbulatov, confirmed it again: "The press should not please itself by an illusion that it is the fourth branch of government. You do not mean anything!"[1] He told us everything about the interrelation between the media and state power. It is now post-perestroika, but still pre-democracy.

NOTE

1. *Izvestiya*, April 1, 1992.

SELECTED BIBLIOGRAPHY

Bungs, Dzintra. Towards Independent Journalism in Latvia? Report on the USSR. Radio Liberty. April 14, 1989.

Culture and the Media in the USSR Today. Ed. by Julian Graffy and Geoffrey A. Hosking. The McMillan Press Ltd. Houndmills, Basingstoke, Hampshire and London, 1989.

Dizard, Wilson P., and Swensrud S. Blake. *Gorbachev's Information Revolution. Controlling Glasnost in a New Electronic Era.* Center for Strategic and International Studies. Westview Press. Boulder, Colorado, 1987.

Dobbs, Michael. Workers of the World, Fax! *The Washington Post*, December 23, 1990.

Dufresne, Marcel. A Soviet Press Code. *Washington Journalism Review*, July/August 1990.

Eribo, Festus, Stephen Vaughn and Hayg Oshagan. The Changing Media in the USSR: New Evidence from a Recent Survey. *Gazette*, No. 45, 1990.

Finlay, Marike. Assessing the contribution to democracy of new communications technology. *Media Development*, March 1989.

Is Censorship Gone? Ambiguities Remain. *The Current Digest of the Soviet Press*, Vol. XLII, No. 42, 1990.

Keller, Bill. For a Soviet Military Editor, Battling Changes, Even Hitler Serves the Cause. *The New York Times*, January 7, 1991.

———. The People's Paper Feeds on Facts and Gets Fat. *The New York Times*, March 3, 1989.

———. Izvestia Opens Pages to "Parasites." *The New York Times*, January 4, 1989.

———. An Editor's Cry from Gorbachev's Doghouse. *The New York Times*, October 24, 1989.

Laptev, Ivan. Soviet Journalists on the Eve of Radical Changes. *The Democratic Journalist*, June 1990.

Lauristin, Marju, and Peeter Vihalem. Estonian Mass Media: Past, Present and

Future. *European Journal of Communication*, Vol. 5, No. 4, December 1990.

Mass Culture and Perestroika in the Soviet Union. *Journal of Communication*, Spring 1991, Vol. 41, No. 2.

Mitchel, Alison. Soviet Newspaper as Glasnost Symbol. *Newsday*, October 25, 1989.

―――. Russian Editors feel Glasnost Chill. *Newsday*, November 24, 1989.

―――. Editor of Pravda out, Gorbachev ally's in. *Newsday*, October 20, 1989.

Peterson, D. J. Medicines, Newspapers and Protecting the Environment. Report on the USSR. Radio Liberty. March 23, 1990.

Pittman, Riitta H. Perestroika and Soviet Cultural Politics: The Case of the Major Literary Journals. *Soviet Studies*, Vol. 42, No. 1, January 1990.

Politics and the Soviet System. Essays in Honour of Frederick C. Barghoorn. Edited by Thomas F. Remington. St. Martin's Press, New York, 1989.

Remnick, David. Chapligin Street Blues. *The New York Review of Books*, April 25, 1991.

Shogren, Elisabeth. Izvestia Staff Protests Plan to Transfer Senior Editor. *Los Angeles Times*, January 21, 1991.

Schmemann, Serge. Soviet TV Reflects the Kremlin's Grimmer Picture. *The New York Times*, February 8, 1991.

Tolz, Vera. Adoption of the Press Law: A New Situation for the Soviet Media? Report on the USSR. Radio Liberty. July 6, 1990.

―――. Central Media Wage Propaganda Campaign Against Lithuania. Report on the USSR. Radio Liberty. April 13, 1990.

―――. Controversy over Draft Law on the Press. *Radio Free Europe/Radio Liberty*. Radio Liberty Research. December 6, 1988.

―――. The development of Glasnost' in 1988. Report on the USSR. Radio Liberty. February 3, 1989.

―――. The Impact of the New Press Law: A Preliminary Assessment. Report on the USSR. Radio Liberty. November 9, 1990.

―――. Soviet Journalists Are Given New Instructions. Radio Free Europe/Radio Liberty. Radio Liberty Research. January 13, 1988.

Wishnevsky, Julia. Censorship in These Days of Glasnost. Radio Free Europe/Radio Liberty. Radio Liberty Research. November 3, 1988.

―――. Press Law Makes Trouble for Writers' Union. Report on the USSR. Radio Liberty. November 2, 1990.

Yasmann, Victor. Direct Broadcasting Satellites: The Search for a New Approach in the USSR. Radio Free Europe/Radio Liberty. Radio Liberty Research. June 6, 1988.

―――. Direct Satellite Broadcasting in the USSR: Is the Time Coming? Report on the USSR. Radio Liberty. May 12, 1990.

―――. Glasnost versus Freedom of Information: Political and Ideological Aspects. Report on the USSR. Radio Liberty. July 21, 1989.

―――. Soviet Television after Glasnost. Report on the USSR. Radio Liberty. November 9, 1990.

INDEX

About the Author

ELENA ANDROUNAS is the owner and director of Comcon, a communications consulting company in Moscow. Previously, she has held positions at Moscow University, the Annenberg School of Communications of the University of Pennsylvania, and the Freedom Forum Media Studies Center at Columbia University.